THE STORY OF

AIR TRANSPORT

IN AMERICA

· CONNECTING · A · CONTINENT ·

THE STORY OF

AIR TRANSPORT
IN AMERICA

**Ray Spangenburg
and Diane K. Moser**

The Story of Air Transport in America
Copyright © 1992 by Ray Spangenburg and Diane K. Moser

Facts On File, Inc.
460 Park Avenue South
New York, NY 10016
USA

Facts On File Limited
c/o Roundhouse Publishing Ltd.
P.O. BOX 140
Oxford OX2 75F
United Kingdom

Library of Congress Cataloging-in-Publication Data
Spangenburg, Ray, 1939–
The story of air transport in America / Ray Spangenburg and Diane K. Moser.
p. cm. — (Connecting a continent)
Includes bibliographical references and index.
Summary: Examines the history of air transport in the United States, from the Wright brothers to modern jets.
ISBN 0-8160-2260-7
1. Aeronautics—United States—History—Juvenile literature.
[1. Aeronautics—History.] I. Moser, Diane, 1944– . II. Title.
III. Series: Spangenburg, Ray, 1939– Connecting a continent.
TL521.S83 1992
629.13—dc20   91-38051

A British CIP catalogue record for this book is available from the British Library.

Facts On File books are available at special discounts when purchased in bulk quantities for businesses, associations, institutions or sales promotions. Please call our Special Sales Department in New York at 212/683-2244 (dial 800/322-8755 except in NY, AK or HI) or in Oxford at 865/728399.

Text and Jacket design by Donna Sinisgalli
Composition by Facts On File, Inc./Grace Ferrara
Manufactured by the Maple-Vail Book Manufacturing Group
Printed in the United States of America

10 9 8 7 6 5 4 3 2 1

In memory of Raymond Spangenburg, Sr.,
restless pilot, dreamer and lover of life

CONTENTS

ACKNOWLEDGMENTS

We'd like to thank the many individuals, too numerous to name, who helped us on this project. We greatly appreciated both their aid and enthusiasm. Several made special contributions, going out of their way to supply photos and help make this book better, including: Tim Kronin and Don Hagedorn at the Air and Space Museum and Ned Perella at the Smithsonian Institution; Harry Gann, Archivist, Douglas Aircraft Company; Craig Martin of the Boeing Company; and Barbara Hanson at United Air Lines. A special thanks also to our editor at Facts On File, James Warren, for his many insightful suggestions in shaping this series.

THE STORY OF

AIR TRANSPORT

IN AMERICA

1

A DREAM OF WINGS: A BRIEF HISTORY OF EARLY ATTEMPTS AT FLIGHT

At this very moment, thousands of airplanes, large and small, commercial and private, are taking off or landing somewhere around the world. Today over 500 commercial airlines carrying passengers and cargo operate daily around the globe. More than 9,000 airplanes, of which over 6,000 are jet powered, fly for these airlines, and one major American airline alone schedules more than 1,900 departures every 24 hours, carrying a daily average of over 150,000 passengers. Each year in the United States more than 400 million people travel with the nation's major airlines. Tens of thousands of private airplanes also take to the air each day. In fact, over 90% of all the registered aircraft in the United States are classified as "general aviation," or noncommercial aircraft. Operating either for business or pleasure, these smaller planes range from sleek private jets carrying executives or celebrities to simpler, propeller-driven aircraft flown by "flying veterinarians," ranchers, farmers, crop dusters, small-business people, flying buffs and hobbyists.

Around the world too, each day thousands of military aircraft take to the skies, from gigantic cargo and troop carriers to streaking fighter jets, "spy planes" and general transportation aircraft.

No one is surprised to hear the sound of engines high overhead or to look up and see the sunlight glinting off a faraway pair of sleek metal wings. And no heads turn in wonder when people say that they have to meet a friend, loved one or business associate "at the airport."

And yet only a little more than 100 years ago the commonplace flights of today were considered only a dream, a science-fiction fantasy fit only for the very young, the very foolish and those people throughout history who have made so many such dreams come true—the inventors, engineers, adventurers and dreamers.

The history of the dream, though, goes back much farther than 100 years. It probably began with the first humans who watched birds in flight and envied their airborne freedom and graceful movement. Almost inevitably, those with curious and inventive minds tried to imitate them. One of the most famous of all Greek myths recounts how the inventor Daedalus fashioned wings of wax and bird feathers so that he and his son, Icarus, could escape from the wrath of King Minos by flying across the sea. Icarus, though, disregarding his father's warnings, flew too high and too close to the sun. With his father watching in horror, the boy's wings disintegrated and he fell to his death. Although the story of Daedalus and Icarus is only a myth, a tale that never actually happened,

Leonardo da Vinci's design for a flying machine. Smithsonian Institution   PHOTO NO. 87-15490

history also tells of many ancient would-be fliers who died or were seriously injured while trying to fly like the birds.

Leonardo da Vinci, the great artist and engineering genius of the 15th and 16th centuries, was the first to leave detailed drawings of mechanical flying devices that demonstrated a more scientific approach to the problems of flight. But 250 years earlier another thinker, a Franciscan monk named Roger Bacon, also envisioned a balloonlike contraption filled with some substance that would be lighter than air, providing a way to float a person up into the skies. Bacon, though, had no idea just what substance would do this.

The French poet and adventurer Savinien de Cyrano de Bergerac made an imaginative suggestion in his stories *Voyages to the Moon and the Sun*, published in 1657 and 1662. Dew rising in the morning air, Cyrano fantasized, could be captured in a glass ball, buoying it upward and lifting its passengers into the air. No one knows whether he was merely joking or not, but by the 18th century a good many inventors were trying to solve the problems of balloon flight for real.

And then suddenly, one summer in Paris, France the skies were filled with men and women riding balloons. "Balloonomania" had hit the nation. Brightly colored balloons, large and small, with passenger-carrying baskets attached, floated over the Paris rooftops. After centuries of dreams, people were "flying" at last.

THE MONTGOLFIER BALLOON

It had all started when two brothers, Joseph and Étienne Montgolfier, noticed that scraps of paper drifted upward from the fire burning in their fireplace. Being papermakers by profession, the Montgolfiers began experimenting with paper bags, turning the open end downward to catch the rising air from the fireplace. The bags, too, rose and drifted upward. The brothers speculated that perhaps the burning fire was releasing some kind of special gas. Actually, the heated air had become rarefied, or less dense. As it was now lighter than the cold air surrounding it, the air carried the paper upward. The next step was obvi-

2

On November 21, 1783 Jean François Pilâtre de Rozier and the Marquis d'Arlandes made the first aerial journey across Paris in a balloon like this one. Scribner's Monthly, February 1871

ous. On October 15, 1783, using a large, paper-lined linen bag filled with their special "Montgolfier gas," the two brothers successfully launched their first human-carrying balloon. A long rope tethered to the ground kept the passenger, a man named Pilâtre de Rozier, safe from flying. But "fly" he did. And soon the Paris skies were filled with untethered free-flying hot-air balloons carrying delighted air travelers.

Of course, with no means of "steering" and no control over the prevailing winds, the whole adventure in those early days of balloon travel was simply a joy ride. The passengers had to trust in fate for a pleasant flight and destination. So humans at last were "in the air," observed an unimpressed critic watching one of the Montgolfier brothers' demonstrations, but of what use was it? The answer came in the form of a question from an American standing beside him who happened to be visiting Paris at the time. "What use is a newborn baby?" Benjamin Franklin rejoined.

With the balloon mania spreading over Europe, people soon improved on the Montgolfiers' simple hot-air balloon. The first major change was the switch to filling the balloon with hydrogen gas, which had recently been discovered. Hydrogen is naturally lighter than air, and using it in balloons removed the danger of carrying a lighted fire aboard to keep the balloon afloat. Still, though, many dreamers weren't satisfied with simple "ballooning." It was nice, and even fun, but still, these dreamers argued, no one was actually flying with the graceful freedom and control of the birds. No one yet could soar with total, controlled power, glide, dip, take off and land at will, or travel as masters of the skies rather than as passive passengers at the whim of the winds.

2

IT ALL BEGAN AT KITTY HAWK: THE EARLY DAYS OF FLYING IN AMERICA

By the end of the 19th century, with the success of lighter-than-air craft clearly established, the early pioneers of flight turned their attention once again toward the problems of constructing a controllable heavier-than-air craft that could carry humans on sustained flights. A few of these pioneers began to take a new look at the graceful dips and glides of birds that soar, such as hawks, gulls and the albatross. Perhaps, they reasoned, humans could not emulate the birds' flapping wings to achieve powered flight, but what about the fixed and stable positions of those wings during these birds' long and graceful glides? Out of such a simple change in perspective came the next great step toward today's modern world of flight.

The world had changed a lot since the day the Montgolfier brothers launched their first successful balloon flight carrying a human into the Paris skies. Steam power had brought an industrial revolution to England, much of Europe and the United States. Machines introduced into every industry, from mining to manufacturing to farming, changed both the way people worked and the way they lived. Transportation in the United States was transformed by steamboats that could travel upriver, by canals that could carry bulk goods cheaply and, most of all, by railroads that connected nearly every section of the continent with ribbons of steel. The first transcontinental railroad, completed in 1869, was soon followed by others

to the north and south. Feeder lines carried grains, meat and other produce to urban markets and returned with supplies and manufactured goods for the farmers. And the 1890s would see the birth of the automobile and yet another transportation revolution. Liberated from the horse and buggy and the railroad track, Americans would begin to travel—and their vast country began to seem smaller, more connected and more integrated than ever.

Keeping pace, the air pioneers continued their heroic and often lonely quest. But in spite of the daily technological miracles that were transforming their lives, most people still believed the day was far off, if indeed it would ever come, when humans would truly conquer the skies.

LILIENTHAL'S GLIDER

In England in the early 1800s, George Cayley had begun a serious investigation into the aerodynamics of gliders. He carefully wrote up his results and successfully flew a few gliders with human passengers aboard for short periods in 1809. And in the United States, John J. Montgomery, a California college professor, made a series of successful flights in the last half of the 19th century before being killed in a glider crash near San Diego in 1911. Others around the world, too, were beginning to

Otto Lilienthal testing out his glider before a crowd of onlookers. Smithsonian Institution   PHOTO NO. A 30908A

add their knowledge to glider designs. The greatest of the glider pioneers, though, was a German, Otto Lilienthal.

Born in Auklam, Prussia in 1848, Lilienthal had been fascinated with the problems of flight since childhood. But it was not until after the Franco-Prussian war (1870–71), in which he served, that he had a chance to put his theories about gliders into action. One of his earliest innovations was to add a curve to the wings of his first glider, which he successfully flew unmanned in 1877. In 1891 he climbed aboard one of his experimental gliders himself and made his first successful flight. It was the beginning of an incredible series of over 2,000 flights that Lilienthal would make over the next five years before dying of injuries from a crash in 1896. (Lilienthal's last words were "Sacrifices must be made.")

His work was not in vain. Hundreds of others, inspired by his flights, had designed their own gliders, and by the turn of the century "gliding" had become almost as popular an activity as ballooning had been 100 years earlier. Still, though, gliders weren't the true "flying machines" that so many early enthusiasts had envisioned. Humans now "had wings." But what was still needed was a way to make gliders more stable (many crashed and injured or killed people) and to add a means of propulsion that would allow them to fly under their own power rather than the power of the wind.

NOT IN A THOUSAND YEARS

Samuel Pierpont Langley, an American, was one of many ingenious people working worldwide on those problems. A truly remarkable man, Langley was one of the breed of "rugged individualists" that America seemed to be producing in abundance in the late 1800s. Born in Massachusetts in 1834, Langley never went to college but nonetheless carved out a solid reputation as a successful civil engineer and architect. A self-taught astronomer, he was appointed to the position of assistant in astronomy at Harvard University in 1865. By 1887 he had received appointments in astronomy at numerous schools and had accepted a position at the Smithsonian Institution.

Despite his varied interests, it was the problem of powered heavier-than-air flight that intrigued Langley the most. And, before the Wright brothers, he probably came closer than anyone to solving that problem.

Highly dedicated and disciplined, Langley was in his fifties when he began to upscale to full size the small glider models he had been working on for years. He had carefully studied aerodynamics and how different wing shapes and structures were affected by the air, and now he applied what he had learned. His ambition was not only to build a more stable and controllable glider but, more important, to fit an engine to it that would allow his "aerodrome," as he called it, to carry passengers in controlled and powered flight.

Major Events in Air Travel

1793–1911

1793 January 9. First public balloon ascent in the United States, made by Pierre Blanchard at Philadelphia.

1861 First military reconnaissance from a balloon in the United States, Arlington, Virginia.

1896 May 6. Flight demonstration with a steam-powered model aircraft (not full size) by Samuel Langley of the Smithsonian Institution.

Octave Chanute begins improving on Lilienthal's glider designs in hang-glider experiments in Chicago.

1902 The Wright brothers make over 700 glider trials on the sand dunes of Kitty Hawk, North Carolina.

1903 December 17. The Wright brothers succeed in making the first controlled and sustained powered flight at Kitty Hawk.

1908 February 10. The Wright brothers receive the first U.S. military contract ever given for an airplane.

1910 November 14. Eugene Ely, a Curtiss test pilot, takes off and lands from the deck of a U.S. military ship, the USS *Birmingham.*

1911 January 26. Glenn Curtiss makes the first successful flight in a displacement-pontoon seaplane, at San Diego, California.

September 17–December 10. Calbraith P. Rodgers flies coast to coast in a contest proposed by publisher William Randolph Hearst. Rodgers flies 3,390 miles from Sheepshead Bay, New York, but reaches Pasadena, California 19 days past the deadline and the Pacific Ocean more than a month later.

His theories were good, and in 1896 one of his full-size craft actually flew "pilotless" for a brief time. The biggest problem Langley faced was finding structural materials for the craft that were lightweight and strong enough, or engines that were small and light enough, to also allow his aerodrome to carry the additional weight of a human.

Despite popular skepticism and much ridicule from the press, Langley was able to get the United States government to invest $50,000 in his research. He used the money to finance three separate trials between 1897 and 1903. Unfortunately, all three failed—the last with the additional humiliation of a *New York Times* editorial scoffing at his research and at the government's foolish use of funds for such hair-brained projects. Moreover, the newspaper predicted, man would not succeed in flying in such contraptions in 1,000 years! The ridicule, on top of the failure, was too much for Langley. Disheartened, at age 69, he abandoned his quest.

Ironically, only nine days after the *Times* article appeared, two brothers rolled their latest invention onto the sand dunes at Kitty Hawk, North Carolina and made history.

SUCCESS AT KITTY HAWK

The Wright brothers were not an overnight success story. Although popular stories often picture them as bicycle builders and part-time inventors who managed to tinker the world's first true flying machine together, Wilbur and Orville Wright were both longtime believers in flight. They were also hard-working and careful builders. Familiar with what other pioneers had attempted and accomplished before them, they had studied long and hard, mastered the available literature and knowledge of aerodynamics, and built their craft carefully and slowly.

Flyer, as the Wright brothers optimistically called their airplane, had not been built on a whim. Three years before their successful flight at Kitty Hawk, Wilbur Wright had written to another flight pioneer, Octave Chanute:

The Wright Brothers—First to Fly

Nearly everyone in the 1890s had or wanted to have a bicycle. Cyclists toured the countryside in groups. Cycling clubs formed and lobbied (successfully) for better roads. And the bicycle took America by storm. So the bicycling business was a natural for two mechanically inclined young brothers. Orville and Wilbur Wright, still in their early 20s, set up shop next door to their home in Dayton, Ohio and began building bicycles in 1892. They were honest and forthright—qualities their customers appreciated—and bicycle enthusiasts from all over town soon gave them a brisk business.

But they'd never forgotten their fascination with flight, begun 14 years earlier when their father, United Brethren Bishop Milton Wright, gave them a toy helicopter. They approached the problem scientifically, not just by trial and error, but also by studying principles. Control by the pilot was a key to success, and they experimented long and hazardously with methods for warping the wing and control with a rudder. On their famous first flight, Orville Wright controlled their aircraft, the *Flyer*, by using a combination of rudder movements and wing warp—lying on his stomach on the bottom wing of the biplane and changing the warp of the wing by rocking in a cradle beneath his hips.

After studying meteorological charts and wind conditions, the brothers had chosen the windswept sand dunes of Kitty Hawk, North Carolina for their first flight—especially ideal since the Wrights constructed their biplanes with skids, not wheels. On takeoff, the plane's skids were carried on a trolley that ran along a prepared wooden track or launching rail. Handling trucks supported the wings on either side when the craft was not on the runway.

After waiting for weeks for a break in the weather, Wilbur Wright won the toss for the first flight. But he lost out in the history books when *Flyer* plowed into a sand dune. And so, on December 17, 1903, Wilbur ran alongside the plane, supporting the wing until the plane took off. Orville Wright headed *Flyer* into a blustery, cold, 25-mph wind, and flew 120 feet at an air speed of 30 mph—just a short hop, but true flight nonetheless. In three more flights that day Wilbur flew 175 feet, Orville 200 feet, and finally Wilbur flew 59 seconds and 852 feet, the longest flight of the day.

In 1904 the Wright brothers flew their plane in a 90-acre pasture outside of Dayton. *Flyer No. 2*, with improved rudders and engine, could sustain flight for five minutes and do turns and circles. Twice that year the Wrights invited reporters to come see what they were doing. But the engines failed to start both times. There's some evidence that the Wrights, who preferred to experiment in private, rigged the failures to discourage public interest—at least until they were ready.

In 1908 they wowed Europeans with a demonstration in Le Mans, France. By the end of that year they had logged 36 hours 20 minutes of flight time—about six times the records of all other aviators combined. Also in 1908 the U.S. government contracted with the Wrights to build an aircraft that could fly 40 mph and travel 125 miles with a pilot and passenger aboard. In the following year the two brothers incorporated the American Wright Company.

The Wrights' planes, unfortunately, included a few design elements that blocked the brothers from developing much further—since they were reluctant to change a design that worked. Four years later, on May 30, 1912, Wilbur Wright died of typhoid. By 1914 his brother left the business. Although he consulted for the Aviation Service of the Army Signal Corps during World War I, he concentrated primarily on private research. He died on January 30, 1948.

That same year, on the 45th anniversary of the first controlled, powered flight ever made by humans, *Flyer No. 1* was hung in the Smithsonian Institution. And the Wrights, who built and flew it, will always remain the first and greatest name in the history of flight.

Wilbur Wright (r.) watches his brother Orville take off on the first powered flight ever made by a man-carrying, heavier-than-air flying machine, December 17, 1903. Smithsonian Institution   PHOTO NO. 85-18337

For some years I have been afflicted with the belief that flight is possible to man. My disease has increased in severity and I feel that it will soon cost me an increased amount of money if not my life. . . . It is possible to fly without motors, but not without knowledge or skill. This I conceive to be fortunate, for man, by reason of his greater intellect, can more reasonably hope to equal birds in knowledge, than to equal nature in the perfection of her machinery.

Wilbur Wright was born on April 16, 1867 near Millville, Indiana. His brother Orville was born in Dayton, Ohio on August 19, 1871. Their father was a minister whose gift to them of a toy "helicopter," made of bamboo, paper and cork and powered by a wound-up rubber band, began their long odyssey toward that day at Kitty Hawk. They had a business making bicycles (and operating a small local newspaper), but their dream was to develop a "flying machine."

"Those who tried to study the science of aerodynamics knew not what to believe," Wilbur wrote of those early days before their success. "Things which seemed reasonable were very often found to be untrue, and things which seemed unreasonable were sometimes true. Under this condition of affairs students were accustomed to pay little attention to things that they had not personally tested."

Pragmatic and patient, the brothers approached the two major problem areas that faced the early flight pioneers: the stability of the aircraft and a means to power it. Lilienthal had attempted to keep the aircraft stable by continuously shifting his weight to the right or the left as he glided through the air. But the results were jerky and unsatisfactory. Working with hundreds of small models and testing them in flight, the Wright brothers finally hit upon a system that allowed them to alternately "warp" the end of each wing at will to maintain stability in flight. This innovation later evolved to become the movable aileron. To test their ideas, the brothers built their own small wind tunnel, trying out over 200 different wing models before settling on the arrangement that worked best. It was a major breakthrough, and, more important, it also worked with the full-size model that they quickly scaled up. During the fall of 1902, the brothers made over 700 successful glides over the sands of Kitty Hawk.

The next step was to power the craft. To solve the power problem, the brothers turned to the newly perfected internal combustion engine, which used gasoline as fuel. They designed a four-cylinder model that was small and light enough to be fitted on the airplane, and it gave enough power for its size to operate the plane carrying the weight of a passenger.

The first airborne test of the engine-powered plane came on December 15, 1903 when, using a wooden launching rail for a runway, the brothers sent the *Flyer* pilotless into the air. It wasn't an auspicious beginning. The plane rose steeply, the engine stalled, and *Flyer* hurled to the ground. Fortunately, the damage wasn't too bad and the brothers were already experienced in quick repairs. Two days later they were ready to try again.

At 10:30 in the morning on December 17, 1903, a bitter cold and overcast day at Kitty Hawk, North Carolina, the dream of centuries came true. With Orville Wright at the controls, *Flyer* sped down the launching rail for nearly 40 feet and then took to the air! It wasn't a high flight, only a scant 10 feet off of the ground, and it wasn't a long one, lasting only 12 seconds and covering 120 feet. But at last a human truly flew a heavier-than-air, powered and controlled aircraft. Wilbur took it up next. Then Orville made another flight. The fourth and final flight of the day covered nearly half a mile. While the brothers were preparing for yet another trial, a sudden wind squall flipped the plane over as it sat on the ground, causing slight damage and ending the day's work. But a barrier had been broken that morning, and the world was changed forever.

There wasn't a lot of applause, and although one of the five onlookers snapped a picture, only a few brief lines appeared in the newspapers to announce to the world what had happened. But a floodgate had been opened. Within a year others had begun to build their own "flying machines," and by 1905 Orville,

piloting *Flyer 3*, stayed airborne in controlled and powered flight for over half an hour. By 1908 Wilbur had made over 200 flights, often staying in the air for over two hours at a time, and carrying a total of over 60 passengers. The age of the airplane had arrived.

Curiously, though, there were still many who asked the same question posed to Benjamin Franklin in Paris over 100 years before: "Of what use is it?" Americans particularly were skeptical. With the vast U.S. network of railroads meeting most transportation needs, and the new canal being built in Panama to speed up east–west sea route shipping, it was pretty hard to see how the risky little puddle-jumping toy would ever remain anything more than just that—a toy. Much more interesting to many Americans was the new Model T automobile that Henry Ford began turning out in Detroit in 1908. Now that was a gadget with possibilities.

In the meantime, the early aviation pioneers were busy expanding the airplane's limits. In 1909 the French aviator Louis Blériot flew across the English Channel. Almost immediately thereafter he received over 200 orders from other would-be flyers asking him to build similar airplanes for them. In 1910 the American aviation pioneer Glenn Curtiss, who had started

The Wright brothers and their biplanes opened the age of flight. By 1908 Wilbur had made over 200 flights, some lasting more than two hours at a time. Smithsonian Institution PHOTO NO. 86-14843

Glenn H. Curtiss:
Early Aircraft Builder and Flight Pioneer

Like the Wright brothers, Glenn Curtiss began as a bicycle builder. Born in Hammondsport, New York on May 21, 1878, he worked as a telegraph messenger boy and for the Eastman Kodak Company in Rochester, New York before opening his first bicycle shop back home in Hammondsport. Lean and muscular, Curtiss was a champion bicycle racer as well as a builder, and in 1907 he set a land speed record for bicycles at Ormond Beach, Florida. By then his reputation as a bicycle builder and racer had spread, and his small shop had expanded to include the manufacture of motorcycles, which were quickly gaining in popularity.

Curtiss's attention, though, turned increasingly toward the skies. Responding to a request from the colorful "Captain Tom Baldwin," a circus performer and parachute jumper who wanted to carry his daredevil exploits into the profitable exhibition circuit, Curtiss built an engine for Baldwin's dirigible, *California Arrow*, which took the top prize in the 1904 Louisiana Purchase Exposition. Following up on that success, Curtiss secured a contract to produce a lighter-than-air craft of his own design, *Dirigible Number One*, for the United States Army. In 1907 he accepted a position as director of experimental work in aeronautics for the Aerial Experiment Association, founded by Alexander Graham Bell, and was soon experimenting with powered heavier-than-air machines.

His first airplane, called the *June Bug*, won a prize offered by the magazine *Scientific American* in 1908 and in 1909 he captured the same prize again. He repeated in 1910 and also won a $10,000 prize awarded by the *New York World* for a flight from Albany to New York City.

Curtiss was quick to realize the military applications of airplanes. One of his biplanes successfully landed on the deck of the USS *Birmingham* in 1910, and he was a major pioneer in seaplanes, selling many of his biplanes to the United States Navy.

Despite a long and drawn-out battle with the Wright brothers over patents, the Curtiss Aeroplane and Motor Company, which he founded, became one of the nation's premier airplane builders. The company boomed during World War I, when it built over 5,000 biplanes for the military, many of which were used in army and navy flight training schools established by Curtiss. Three years after his death in 1930, Curtiss was posthumously awarded the Distinguished Flying Cross for his contributions to military aviation.

experimenting with airplanes under the sponsorship of another pioneer inventor, Alexander Graham Bell, began fitting pontoons to some of his growing stable of airplanes, allowing them to take off and land on the water. And in that same year the forward-thinking Curtiss gave the world a brief and important glimpse of the future when one of his planes, piloted by Eugene Ely, successfully took off from and landed on the deck of a U.S. military ship, the USS *Birmingham*.

THE WACKY FLIGHT OF THE *VIN FIZ*

Another first, even though somewhat zany by today's standards, was given to the world in 1911 by an intrepid flier named Calbraith Rodgers. It all began when newspaper publisher William Randolph Hearst announced a prize of $50,000 for the first pilot to make a flight across the United States in 30 days.

"Cal," as he liked to be called, decided to try for it. A cigar-chomping, six-foot-four aviator with his eye on glory, Cal Rodgers held flying license number 49 (there were only 50 legally licensed pilots in the United States at the time). He had already won an $11,000 prize at one of the nation's first "air meets" at Chicago and was now looking around for a bigger challenge. In an effort to prove the worth of the new machines, others had started making long-distance flights: Pierre Prier flew nonstop from London to Paris in under four hours; a Curtiss plane made the trip from Key West, Florida 90 miles over water to Havana, Cuba; and H. N. Atwood had flown a Wright biplane from St. Louis to New York via Chicago. So why, the ambitious Cal Rodgers reasoned, couldn't someone make a transcontinental flight? Hearst himself doubted that anyone would walk off with his award, and Orville Wright had even gone on record as saying that the flight was ". . . impossible. The machine has not been made yet that can do it!" But Rodgers, with only two months of flying experience under his belt, decided to give it a try.

To round up financial backing, he made a deal with Armor and Co. to drop leaflets along his way advertising their new grape-flavored soft drink, Vin Fiz. Then he chose a $5,000 modified Wright biplane to do the job. The plane was incredibly fragile, even with Rodgers's extra wire supports and modifications. Its four-cylinder, 40-horsepower engine could manage about 45 miles an hour with the wind, but the plane was hardly more than a glorified box kite with an engine and propellers. Since there would obviously have to be many scheduled and unscheduled stops along the way, Rodgers and Armor Co. commissioned a private train (Cal planned to follow railroad tracks along the way to help in navigation). The train, made up of five cars, carried his family and mechanics, along with a doctor and a chauffeur. (Cal liked to travel in style.) Two cars were stocked with spare parts for the biplane and one was a completely outfitted machine shop. Always planning ahead, Rodgers even had an automobile loaded on board—for those unscheduled landings when someone might have to come out and hunt for him.

On September 17, 1911 the biplane, christened the *Vin Fiz* with a bottle of Armor's soft drink, took to the air at Sheepshead Bay Racetrack near New York City. But first Rodgers had to spend two hours on the ground frantically trying to get his plane airborne as he tried to outmaneuver the crowd of over 2,000 who had come to cheer him on his way. That zany and bewildering beginning was to set the stage for the whole trip. The first leg ended at Middletown, New York, where Rodgers touched down for the night in an elated frame of mind.

"I should easily average 200 miles a day cross-continent," he predicted to the waiting crowd and reporters, before slipping into the Pullman car of his waiting train for a hot meal.

It had been a good "hop" and a good landing. Rodgers liked to judge a landing by the ashes still clinging to the end of his cigar after his wheels touched down. But it was one of the few good landings he would make on his long journey.

His trouble started upon takeoff the next morning. A few seconds after leaving the ground, one wheel clipped the top of a tree. The plane went out of control and crashed into a chicken coop, sending feathers flying in all directions. The crowd pulled Cal from the wreckage. He was bleeding and shaken. But the cigar was still in his mouth (the

A typical crowd, waving and cheering to Cal Rodgers during his historic flight in the Vin Fiz. Smithsonian Institution
PHOTO NO. A 3475

With his crutches strapped to the wing, Cal Rodgers grins behind a cigar as his plane's wheels finally dip into the waves of the Pacific on December 10, 1911. Smithsonian Institution PHOTO NO. 77-9038

ashes, presumably, jarred loose). The biplane, however, needed a day and a night of repairs.

Repaired and behind schedule, the *Vin Fiz* took off again, and Rodgers covered another 95 miles westward before touching down for a rest. At take-off, though, he and his repair crew had to fight off a huge crowd of souvenir hunters who attacked in force, stealing parts from the plane. One woman argued, when they caught her unscrewing a nut, "There are so many—one won't make any difference." The rampaging souvenir hunters may have shaken the dignified Rodgers up almost as much as his crash into the chicken coop—when he came down next in Elmira, New York, he discovered that he had flown 215 miles off course.

And Cal's troubles continued. At Red House, near Salamanca, New York, he crashed again, hitting a barbed-wire fence during takeoff and breaking his two propellers, a wing and his landing gear. He then crashed near Huntington, Indiana after trying to fly under some telephone wires. The *Vin Fiz* needed further repairs, but Cal, by now getting used to it, just dusted himself off and grumbled.

There were moments of glory, though. Pallbearers in a funeral procession near Hammond, Indiana set down their coffin and waved jubilantly up at him. Over Joliet Prison he tipped his wings to the assembled prisoners waving from the prison yard.

"I intend to get to the Pacific if it takes me a year," he announced. By Chicago he had been thrown from his plane over a half a dozen times in miscalculated stops on landings and takeoffs. At Muskogee, Oklahoma he crashed again. Over Sanderson, Texas a piston crystallized, and he was forced to make another emergency landing, safely this time. But on takeoff Rodgers crashed into a fence, which pitched him over the top of the plane again and into a muddy pond.

At Fort Hancock, a pump connection sheered off, and his propeller chain snapped near El Paso.

North of Waco, Texas he was attacked by a giant eagle, which chased the plane for miles before forcing Rodgers to land, again with damage to the plane.

The situation was getting out of hand. But Cal only became more determined. To help offset the growing expenses of new parts, Cal's backers began charging

---

Historical Headlines

1891–1911

1892   In Chicago, the first electric automobile (made by William Morrison of Des Moines, Iowa) is driven.

Frank and Charles Duryea of Massachusetts make the first American gasoline-powered automobile.

1894   German inventor Rudolf Diesel invents the Diesel engine.

1898   Spanish-American War begins; the Treaty of Paris is signed in December with the United States emerging as a recognized world power.

William McKinley takes a ride in a Stanley Steamer, becoming the first President to ride in an automobile.

1903   A Packard car travels from San Francisco to New York in 52 days in the first trip across the United States by automobile.

Henry Ford establishes the Ford Motor Company.

The Williamsburg Bridge, over the East River in New York City, becomes the first large suspension bridge to be constructed using steel towers.

1909   The 16th Amendment to the Constitution, granting Congress the power to levy and collect income tax, is sent to the states for ratification.

---

towns along the way $500 for the attraction of scheduled landings. But of course the *unscheduled* ones were usually the most spectacular. Rodgers had lost 15 pounds and the *Vin Fiz* had lost and replaced so many parts that it was almost an entirely different plane from the one he had started with. But both were still flying.

On November 3 the flight almost came to an end near the Salton Sea in California when a cylinder exploded, spiraling the fragile biplane out of control and piercing Rodgers's arm with sharp splinters of steel. Despite excruciating pain, he fought for control of the bucking plane, finally landing safely at Imperial Junction on the Santa Fe Railroad line.

Pasadena, California was now only 178 miles away. By morning, with both Rodgers and the plane patched up again, he ordered his crew to hack down a four-mile path through the sagebrush to give him room for a takeoff. It took six attempts before he cleared the ground.

A crowd of 20,000 people greeted Rodgers and the *Vin Fiz* at Pasadena on November 5, 1911. His flight had taken him past the time limit stipulated for Hearst's

prize, but he was the first flyer to span the country coast to coast.

The trip had taken 49 days, and he had crashed over 70 times, but Cal Rodgers was a hero.

That night he signed the hotel register "C. P. Rodgers—New York to Pasadena by Air." But for him there was still one more short hop to be made. He had promised himself that he was going to fly ocean to ocean, and he intended to dip his wheels into the Pacific.

His luck hadn't gotten any better, though. Taking off the next day for his simple hop to the Pacific, he crashed again! This time he was pulled from the wreckage with two broken legs, a broken collar bone and a brain concussion.

The patch-up job took longer this time, but Rodgers still had a personal vow to keep. Finally, on December 10, 1911, 84 days after he left New York, Cal Rodgers flew to Long Beach, California—a pair of crutches lashed to his airplane wing—and dipped his landing gear into the Pacific.

A study in determined obstinacy and daring, and typical of the early pioneers in aviation, Cal Rodgers made history as the first to cross the United States by air. Unfortunately, his entire flying career lasted less than a year. A few months later, on April 3, 1912, the *Vin Fiz* crashed again with Rodgers at the controls. It was his last flight. Plunging into the ocean, Cal Rodgers died, his back and neck broken, less than 500 yards from where he had triumphantly taxied into the Pacific.

The restored *Vin Fiz* hangs today, along with the Wright brothers' *Flyer* and other historic aircraft, in the Pioneers of Flight Gallery at the Smithsonian's Air and Space Museum in Washington, D.C.

"Of what use was it?" Maybe none. But as Cal Rodgers would have said, somebody had to do it. After waiting so long to be born, aviation was taking its first faltering steps out of its infancy.

3

WORLD WAR I LEAVES A LEGACY: FIGHTER PILOTS, BARNSTORMERS AND AIR MAIL

The airplane grew up fast during the four years of World War I, from 1914 to 1918. Before the war, balloon and dirigible flights had already proved the usefulness of high vantage points for reconnaissance. The military was quick to recognize that airplanes, with their better mobility and control, could do the job even more quickly and efficiently. In 1907 President Theodore Roosevelt had passed a newspaper clipping about a Wright brothers' flight on to one of his assistants with a terse, one-word command: "Investigate." The military became one of the first buyers of a Wright brothers' airplane, and before America entered the war Glenn Curtiss was already demonstrating his machine's military capabilities.

France, still at the forefront of aviation, had put military planes into the air during the first days of the war. And Germany was not only building superior planes to use against the Allies, but it was also building an elite corps of top-notch pilots to fly its expanding air fleet. By the time the United States entered the war against Germany in April 1917, airplanes had proved capable of much more than just flying reconnaissance missions. Fitted out with machine guns capable of firing through the airplane's propellers without damaging them, as well as new and improved means to drop explosive bombs, the new military aircraft were chang-

ing the face of modern warfare. By war's end, England alone was manufacturing over 30,000 planes a year for war use, and its aircraft industry had expanded in four short years from a few small, scattered back-of-the-barn shops to a thriving manufacturing sector employing over 350,000 men and women.

It's often said that World War I made the world more conscious of airplanes, forcing it to take the "toy" more seriously. But the truth is that outside of the military, even after the war most people still thought of the airplane as a fragile, dangerous and impractical way to travel. Curiously, though, the world had become very conscious of the men who did the flying. The exploits of the pilots on both sides of the conflict did much to give the world heroic images and to take its eyes away from the not-so-glorious, bloody and dirty war being fought in the trenches and battlegrounds.

From the Lafayette Escadrille (a group of daredevil and dashing American pilots who joined the French Foreign Legion as fliers early in the war) to Germany's famous Baron Manfred von Richthofen, the world now saw the airplane pilot as a new kind of romantic hero. It took a special breed of person to fly airplanes, it was said. Helped along by tales, often true, of combat codes and chivalry, daring and expertise by both sides during the war, fliers were now seen as dashing "knights of the air,"

Wing Walkers like this one on a barnstorming biplane wowed the crowds in the '20s. Smithsonian Institution PHOTO NO. 87-10381

Arthurian heroes on lonely personal quests, flirting always with glory, excitement, danger and death.

It may have been true. Certainly pilots on both sides of the conflict shared a special camaraderie based on the skills and daring required in this new kind of warfare.

The war between these fliers was just as deadly as the one being fought on the ground, but it was more personal than the often faceless firing in the trenches. Two pilots facing each other in their fragile airplanes, engaging in what amounted to personal duels above the clouds, were bound together in a special fraternity of the skies beyond the deadly animosities of war.

BARNSTORMING FOR PEANUTS

When the war was over, most soldiers returned to their homes and families, farms and businesses. For the fliers, though, there was a different return. "Once flying gets in your blood you can't get rid of it," one told a newspaper reporter shortly after the war. Some did go back to their families and previous jobs. Most who had entered the war as pilots or had learned to fly during the war, however, saw themselves as a new kind of professional: a professional flier. It wasn't a career with much future in those early days after World War I. Like the airplanes abandoned on the airfields, the returning fliers found themselves out of place during peacetime. The skies still called, but, other than the recently formed U.S. air mail service, employing a scant 50 fliers at any one time, no one paid fliers much to answer that call. Many decided to answer anyway, paying *themselves* as best they could. Buying up surplus military airplanes, most of which were going cheap, many of those fliers became "barnstormers" and "flying Gypsies" during one of the most colorful eras of American aviation history.

Often creating a kind of one-man, one-machine circus, barnstormers lived a nomadic life of excitement and adventure. Moving from small town to small town across the American continent, they flew their often rickety aircraft at air shows and exhibitions, country fairs, and town celebrations—anywhere that would draw a crowd. They were there to give the crowd a thrill—with fancy flying, roll-overs, controlled stalls

---

Major Events in Air Travel

1912–1926

1912   January 10. First successful flight in a flying boat, made by Glenn Curtiss in San Diego.

1914   January 1. First scheduled airline service begins operation, from Tampa, Florida across Tampa Bay to St. Petersburg.

1918   May 15. Inauguration of first scheduled air mail service, from New York City to Washington, D.C.

1919   Daily air mail service begins between New York City and Chicago.

         September 8. Scheduled transcontinental air mail service begins.

1923   May 2–3. First nonstop transcontinental flight, 2,520 miles in 36 hours and 4 minutes, made by John Macready and Oakley Kelly in an army Fokker T-2 transport.

1924   April 6–September 24. Two Douglas World Cruisers complete the first flight around the world, starting and ending at Seattle, Washington for a total flight of 27,533 miles. Time in flight: 15 days and 11 hours.

1926   May 9. U.S. Navy Commander Richard E. Byrd and Lieutenant Floyd Bennett fly over the North Pole.

---

and dangerous dives—and for a dollar a flight they would take people up one at a time to give them a taste of the skies. Sometimes barnstormers traveled in small teams—a flyer; a mechanic, if one could be found cheap enough; and sometimes a parachute jumper, or "wing walker." The trick was to keep the airplane patched up and flying somehow, and to make enough money to buy fuel, scrounge cheap spare parts, eat a solid meal and be ready to move on to the next town. Sometimes there would be locally sponsored air races and prize money, and occasionally a side job of dropping leaflets and advertising. Always there was the danger of crackups, badly damaged planes, broken bones and sudden death.

And they weren't always welcome wherever they went. The public liked the show but was wary of the pilots and their crews. Jauntily sporting white scarves and leather jackets, the fliers cut a fine figure in the air and on the air field, but before and after the show they were "outsiders." Wary townspeople saw the barnstormers as people who lived too fast, took too many chances, drank a little too much and flirted too openly with the girls in town. Unfortunately, often the townspeople's evaluations were just. The barnstormers were a "different breed," a special fraternity in their own eyes, outside the habits and conventions of those who had safe jobs and secure homes in the small towns along the way. Sometimes, as was the case with a handsome young barnstormer named Charles Lindbergh, townspeople decided they were "all right," good "clean-living folks" and nondrinkers you could trust in your home, or with your daughter. Usually, though, the town that had applauded their thrilling

High-flying acrobatics. Smithsonian Institution PHOTO NO. 82-3644

William E. Boeing (l.) launched an international mail service from Seattle to Victoria, British Columbia in this home-built seaplane on March 3, 1919. The Boeing Company Archives

exploits the day before heaved a sigh of relief when, like circus people the day after a show, the barnstormers packed up their gear and left town.

THE U.S. POST OFFICE GOES AIR MAIL

Not all the returning World War I fliers quit flying or became barnstormers. As early as 1914 the world's first regularly scheduled air-passenger service opened up along a 22-mile route from Tampa to St. Petersburg, Florida. The service could carry only one passenger at a time and cost $5 for the 23-minute flight. The St. Petersburg and Tampa Airboat Line was a financial failure and lasted only a short time, but other

fliers, airplane builders and businesspeople were beginning to look at what services the airplane could offer. In Michigan in 1919 a group known as the Maycock Flyers began offering nationwide such aircraft services as aerial photography, surveying, crop dusting and emergency passenger flights on an irregular, unscheduled basis. Then in 1920 the first regularly scheduled flight service to a foreign port opened up when a small company called Aeromarine Airways started passenger service between Key West, Florida and Havana, Cuba. Operated by an automobile dealer with the tongue-twisting name of Inglus M. Uppercu, this Key West to Havana line soon opened another short line from Miami to the Bahamas, taking advantage of the wealthy tourist trade. Ever enterprising, Uppercu also began a line between Detroit, Michigan and Cleveland, Ohio beginning in 1922. The flight cost passengers $25 each and took 90 minutes. The same distance took five hours by rail and cost $9, while the still slower steamboat passage could be purchased for $5. Uppercu's growing empire came to an end, though, in 1923 when two of his planes crashed into the shark-infested ocean off the Florida coast. Put off by dramatic newspaper accounts, coupled with the deaths of five passengers on the first crash and four more on the second, Uppercu's investors withdrew, forcing him to close his operation. "You cannot get one nickel for commercial flying," he told reporters when he announced his company's closing.

Other entrepreneurs, however, were not discouraged. By 1925 the *Aircraft Yearbook*, the official publication of the Aeronautical Chamber of Commerce, reported that commercial operators were scattered throughout the United States. Twenty-eight of the fliers who returned the yearbook's query reported

that they flew only for pleasure, but the rest reported such activities as nonregularly scheduled cargo, passenger and mail deliveries. The 290 pilots who responded also reported a total of 676 airplanes, flying collectively over 5,396,672 miles, with 205,094 passengers carried and 112 tons of cargo and mail.

Still, the going was rough for commercial air operations. Some European airline companies, flying both dirigibles and heavier-than-air machines, were able to keep their lines operating with the help of heavy government subsidies. In the United States, no such subsidies were being offered to the fledgling attempts at commercial aviation. The public for the most part still distrusted airplanes—as well as subsidies. Anyway, trains could still take you just about any long distance you wanted to travel, even if they were slower.

But things began to change in 1918 when the United States Post Office Department established its first regularly scheduled air mail service.

Actually, the first mail-carrying flight in the United States was in 1911, when a pilot by the name of Earl

Air mail pilots, flying early planes like this one, affectionately known as the "flying brick," had to peer around various cables, struts and windshields to see where they were going. United Air Lines

Unloading mail and express cargo from a National Air Transport plane at Cleveland in 1928. The man with a shotgun is a postal employee standing guard to make sure the mail goes through as promised. United Air Lines

L. Ovington made several authorized airmail deliveries over a 10-mile area on Long Island, New York. The flights were part of a publicity stunt connected to an air show, but shortly afterward the government began experimenting with other occasional air mail routes and deliveries. With the growing decentralization of many businesses after the war, many businesspeople had shown an interest in faster regularly scheduled mail deliveries. The government, after carefully testing out the concept, decided to give it a regular try.

The inaugural ceremony, held on May 15, 1918, was hardly auspicious, however. The first route to be opened was between New York City, Philadelphia and Washington, D.C. The war was still raging in Europe, and the government promoted its new service not only as an aid to American business but as a valuable training ground for future military pilots. Skeptics doubted that there would be much interest or that the "training" would actually help much in flying combat missions. Ironically, though, some pilots returning home and entering the air mail service after the war would find flying the mail

service just about as dangerous as their combat duties had been.

The opening ceremony, begun in Washington, had already been marred by the botched printing of some of the special 24-cent air mail stamps—with the center of the vignette inverted. Now, with President Woodrow Wilson, his wife and various dignitaries waiting, the mail plane was late in arriving. When at last it showed up and was loaded, it took five attempts to get its engines started again before someone thought to check the fuel tanks. Empty, or nearly so. Finally, after refueling while the president and his party waited patiently, the plane with Lieutenant George Boyle at the controls took to the air and began its first regularly scheduled mail flight. Unfortunately, perhaps due to the confusion and embarrassment on the ground, Boyle took off flying in the wrong direction. Twenty-five miles away, realizing at last what he had done, the pilot was forced to make an unscheduled landing near a Maryland farm.

Critics were also quick to point out at the time that "air mail" actually didn't deliver the mail any faster than first-class rail service along the same route. The planes cruised at only 70 mph and time had to be added for delivering the mail from the post office to the air field and again to a post office at the other end of the line.

But despite its rather questionable beginning, the U.S. Air Mail service soon turned a profit. In August 1918 the Post Office Department took over completely, hiring its own pilots rather than relying on the military. It began an ambitious expansion of its routes and services. By 1920, with the development of relay night flights and lighted air routes, the U.S. Air Mail Service was making coast-to-coast deliveries from New York west to Cleveland, Chicago, Omaha and San Francisco. By 1921 the service was flying westbound in 34 hours and 20 minutes (according to its published schedules) and eastbound in 29 hours and 15 minutes, with six changes of pilots and aircraft en route. The same trip by surface then took four days.

The surprising efficiency of the early air mail service, though, was taking its toll on the health and safety of its pilots. Through a quirk of luck, the early days of the service had been blessed with an unusual spell of good weather. Seeing the chance to win over the skeptics, officials announced that the air mail flights could be conducted on schedule 93% of the time. As the service expanded, however, covering different areas and weather zones, the conditions were much less predictable. Despite this, officials established an efficiency rating system for the pilots, based on the percentage of flights they were able to complete on time.

"It was considered pretty much a suicide club," one early air mail pilot remembered later. Flying in open cockpit biplanes, exposed to the bitterly cold air and harsh weather conditions, the pilots often became so numbed and exhausted that they couldn't think clearly or make decisions quickly. Pushed to make their deadlines, they were forced to take too many chances. The public saw them as daredevils, glamorous and dashing knights of the air risking their

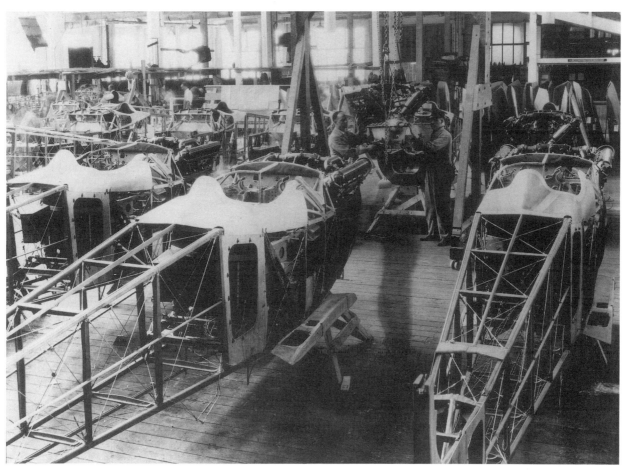

Wood-frame fuselage and cockpit construction at the Boeing aircraft factory in 1922. Smithsonian Institution PHOTO NO. 91-3548

The Ford Trimotor, nicknamed the "Tin Goose," was a modified Stout-AT, the first all-metal air machine. Smithsonian Institution   PHOTO NO. A 268E

lives to get the mail through, but for the pilots themselves flying was often more a matter of nerves and endurance. Not publicized by the Post Office Department was the fact that in order to fight the cold and the constant pressure of deadlines, with on-time delivery expected under even the worst of flying conditions, many of the pilots carried bottles of liquor along when they flew, a habit many continued off duty.

During the midsummer of 1919, one of the worst periods in the history of air mail service, bad weather blanketed most of the East Coast. While officials in Washington pushed for continued flights and strict schedules in order to win the public's confidence, the pilots fought against impenetrable fog, rain and extremely dangerous visibility conditions. Despite Washington's orders, and despite the heroic attempts of the air mail pilots to carry them out, not all the mail did get through on schedule. In one two-week period that summer, 15 planes crashed, injuring a dozen pilots. Two pilots were killed.

By 1925, when the U.S. government began to farm some of its air mail operations out to private airlines, only nine of the original 40 pilots were still alive.

Gradually the air mail system improved. Better scheduling, better flying instruments and better planes began to make flying a lot easier on the pilots. But the improvements didn't come until after much harm had been done, including many injuries and fatalities. On the plus side, many legends about the heroics of the early air mail pilots passed on a legacy of honor and glory to the fliers who followed after them.

FLYING NON-STOP ACROSS THE UNITED STATES

By 1923, only 12 years after Cal Rodgers had made his bizarre 49-day transcontinental flight, the U.S. air mail was regularly making coast-to-coast flights in under 30 hours. The mail service, however, was still using stops and relays along the way. The challenge of long-distance nonstop flights still remained when John Macready and Oakley Kelly decided to attempt the first nonstop flight across the United States. Kelly, a U.S. Air Service officer, and Macready, an officer and test pilot who had recently set a world's record for altitude flying at 4,800 feet, spent months preparing and planning the route and requirements of their flight. Taking off on May 2, 1923 from New York with a box of sandwiches and two thermos bottles filled with coffee and beef broth, Kelly and Macready spelled each other at the front and rear controls of their fuel-heavy Fokker aircraft. They touched down at San Diego, California 26 hours, 50 minutes and 3 seconds later.

The Fokker airplane that Kelly and Macready used for their nonstop transcontinental flight was just one of the many new heavier-than-air machines being manufactured by a dozen companies that emerged during and after World War I. The Fokker had proved its worth during the war, but now many manufacturers were trying to develop machines that had more varied uses.

In 1925 Congress passed the Kelly Act, which turned over mail contracts to private companies. That piece of legislation, along with a major technological breakthrough—the Stout-AT—aircraft, set the stage for the nation's first successful airlines.

The Stout-AT was the world's first all-metal air machine. It replaced the usual configuration, used in most of the other aircraft at the time, in which fabric was stretched over a wooden frame. Designed by inventor William B. Stout, with backing by Henry Ford and the Ford Motor Company, the Stout-AT was modified by the Ford Company after Ford bought Stout

out in 1925. The sturdy little aircraft soon became known as the Ford Trimotor, sometimes nicknamed the "Tin Goose." Much more durable than its competitors, it became the mainstay of many of the emerging airlines in the late 1920s.

By this time, an elaborate system of beacons lit the transcontinental air mail route and well-lighted emergency landing fields every 25 to 30 miles along the way made cross-country flying much safer. Now political pressure mounted for private companies to have a share of the lucrative air mail business. The railroads joined in the campaign, eager to rid themselves of government and competition in long-distance mail transport. And Congress passed the Kelly Act of 1925.

The first air mail contract went to the Ford Motor Company in 1926, but by 1927 a dozen other smaller companies also received postal contracts. Among those first few was Stout Air Services, founded by William Stout, who had continued his air career after selling his manufacturing company to Ford. Coincidentally, the Ford Company, after three years of safe and lucrative mail transport, decided to stick with building planes rather than flying them and turned its mail

Wings of early planes were manufactured by stretching fabric over wooden frames. The Boeing Company Archives

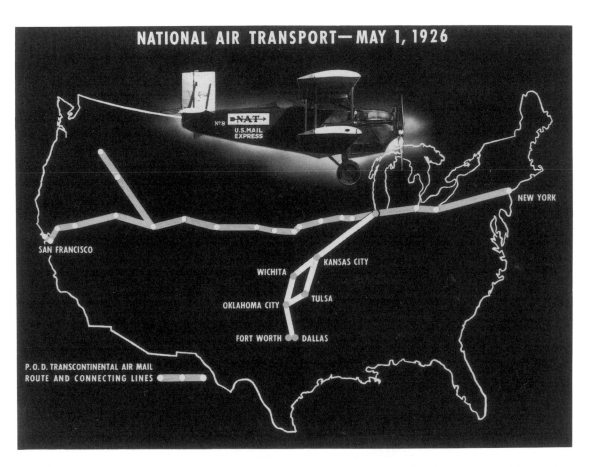

NATIONAL AIR TRANSPORT—MAY 1, 1926

NEW YORK

SAN FRANCISCO

WICHITA

KANSAS CITY

OKLAHOMA CITY

TULSA

FORT WORTH DALLAS

P.O.D. TRANSCONTINENTAL AIR MAIL
ROUTE AND CONNECTING LINES

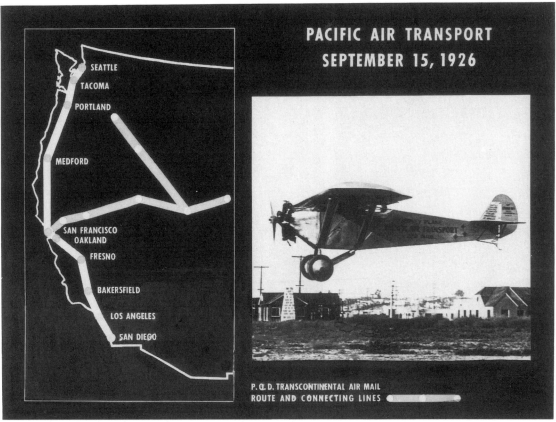

PACIFIC AIR TRANSPORT
SEPTEMBER 15, 1926

SEATTLE

TACOMA

PORTLAND

MEDFORD

SAN FRANCISCO
OAKLAND

FRESNO

BAKERSFIELD

LOS ANGELES

SAN DIEGO

P.O.D. TRANSCONTINENTAL AIR MAIL
ROUTE AND CONNECTING LINES

By 1926 National Air Transport covered the New York to San Francisco route, with service to the Midwest and Texas as well. Pacific Air Transport serviced the north–south route along the West Coast. Later the two would merge to form United Air Lines. United Air Lines

Air Fields in the 1920s

Passenger service began in the United States with a flying boat, but when the U.S. government started to set up air mail service in the 1920s, air fields became important for the first time. These were basically big grassy fields, with two runways of about 2,500 feet each, laid out at right angles to each other. Cargo was wheeled out to waiting aircraft on wheelbarrows or handtrucks, and passengers usually walked across the grassy stubble to clamber into the small planes. Signals for takeoff and landing were often given by a man waving a flag on the runway. To light the pilot's way at night, a powerful beacon light typically revolved on a tower, while emergency landing fields had much smaller beacon lights to guide pilots in for a landing. Still operating without accurate instruments to gauge air speed, altitude or direction, by 1923 pilots had, however, a marked airway to follow at night—a path of acetylene gas beacons set out below at intervals every three miles along their routes.

The first airport to serve New York City, opened at Newark, New Jersey in 1928, had a 1,600-foot hard-surfaced runway—possibly the first in the world. The Newark Airport also had passenger terminals that doubled as hangars for the aircraft, and in 1930 some 20,000 passengers used its facilities.

Building near the outskirts of cities on cheap, open land, air field developers rarely foresaw that future, more powerful aircraft would need longer runways (now 15,000 feet or more) or that their air fields might become so busy that two runways would no longer suffice. Nor did they realize that the cities they served—encouraged by the very transportation they helped provide—would grow up around them, blocking expansion of the air fields. In the 1920s a large, open pasture, leased or purchased cheaply near the edge of town, was still enough.

An early National Air Transport/United Air Lines airport. United Air Lines

contract over to Stout. The new air mail business helped many contractors survive, but most of them, at least in the East and Midwest, still carried few passengers. Most people still considered air travel dangerous, and besides, for the newly emerging airlines, passenger service was less profitable than carrying the mail. The government was paying $3 a pound for flying its mail a thousand miles. To net a comparable profit per pound for flying a passenger the same distance would require a 150-pound passenger to pay $450, not a price most people could afford at the time.

In the West, though, where distances between cities were greater, and travel conditions less hospitable, a few passenger-carrying airlines were beginning to show a profit. Western Air Express, founded in Los Angeles, began by flying the air mail route from Los Angeles to Salt Lake City, Utah, but quickly expanded to carrying passengers as well. Los Angeles was a popular air mail destination, and within six months the city was receiving or sending nearly 40% of all the air mail in the country. The profit helped Western keep up its passenger service, and by 1929 the company, which later would become Western Airlines, was carrying nearly 22,000 passengers a year.

With government money now available in the form of air mail contracts, dozens of other new companies sprang up throughout the West. Varney Air Lines easily won a contract to fly mail from Elko, Nevada to Boise, Idaho and Pasco, Washington, and then wangled a reroute from Salt Lake City, Utah to Boise and Seattle, Washington, connecting key western trade centers. Pacific Air Transport (PAT) flew from Los Angeles to San Francisco. Not all small western carriers served passengers in the beginning, but many of them—including Varney and PAT—would become the seeds from which today's great airlines would grow.

In 1926 the Air Commerce Act brought uniformity and regulation to U.S. civil aeronautics. As a result, commercial airports were required to install lights and safer landing and emergency fields, and the new legislation provided for federal inspection and licensing of aircraft and pilots. The Air Commerce Act was a milestone in aviation history: It introduced order and safeguards that attracted new businesses and investors into the field of commercial aviation. Air transportation was on the verge of growing up. And the world, it seemed, had begun to get smaller.

Historical Headlines

1912–1921

1912   New Mexico becomes the 47th and Arizona the 48th state. No new states will be admitted until Alaska and Hawaii are admitted to the union in 1958 and 1959 respectively.

1914   World War I breaks out in Europe.

The United States completes the Panama Canal, originally started by the French 33 years before.

1915   German attacks on U.S. ships threaten U.S. noninvolvment in World War I.

1917   The United States declares war on Germany.

1918   President Wilson presents his Fourteen Points that he feels are necessary to peace, which are later accepted; the fighting comes to an end.

1920   The 19th Amendment is ratified, granting the right to vote to women.

1921   World War I is officially declared at an end by Congress, and the United States signs and ratifies treaties.

4

THE "SPIRIT" CATCHES ON: CHARLES LINDBERGH OPENS A NEW ERA

As the decade of the 1920s approached its end the future began to look a little bit brighter for the pioneers of early aviation in America. Harry Guggenheim, who had been a flier during World War I, encouraged his father, the wealthy Daniel Guggenheim, to establish the Guggenheim Fund for the Promotion of Aeronautics. In the late 1920s the fund set up new schools of aeronautical engineering at universities across the nation. The Guggenheim Fund also helped in more mundane ways—such as paying towns located along flight routes to paint their rooftops with place names and brightly colored arrows to mark emergency landing fields.

Financial investors, once nearly impossible to find, slowly began to come forward, so that more and more fledgling airlines were beginning to emerge.

But even though government mail contracts helped many in the aviation business get off the ground, it still wasn't always easy to get the planes in the air. Flying was still a primitive business, and much of it was still being done in less than perfect machines. Typical of the kinds of problems faced by many of the fliers in the late 1920s were those faced by Varney Air Lines—and Varney's rugged ingenuity in solving them was also typical. After securing its government mail contract, Varney quickly discovered that it was difficult to get its underpowered planes up in the rarefied mountain air that made up much of its route. The solution employed by some of Varney's pilots was not designed to encourage the confidence of any prospective passengers. Pilots would first place a heavy cut sapling in front of the wheels of the planes, and then lay another down on the runway a couple of

hundred yards away. Then, returning to their planes, they would climb into the cockpit and gun the engine at full throttle, using the sapling in front of their wheels as a brake. Once the plane had enough power, it would jump the sapling and head down the air field at full speed, where it would hit the second sapling and bounce into the air!

"You learned a lot of tricks to get those crates up in the air and keep them flying," one old air mail pilot observed years later.

One pilot who was learning the tricks in the late 1920s had already put in a stint as a barnstormer and was working for the Robertson Aircraft Corporation as an air mail flier along the St. Louis to Chicago route in 1926. People said that Charles Lindbergh had a "good head on his shoulders." Even during his barnstorming days, while liked and admired by most of the other pilots, he had been something of a loner, though. He didn't drink or "cut up" in the towns as most of the other pilots did, and while he could keep up with the best of them when it came to the kinds of stunt flying that drew the crowds, he wasn't a "hotshot" or risk-taker. Flying the air mail route for Robertson, his reputation was one of a quiet, determined pilot who never lost his head and could get the job done. It was an impression that he had left on people ever since childhood.

Born February 4, 1902, Lindbergh hadn't been an overachiever in his school years. Like his father, who had served in the U.S. Congress from 1907 to 1917 and who owned a small farm in Little Falls, Minnesota, Charles was steadfast, methodical and self-confident. If it could be done, the Lindberghs could do it. Maybe not as fancily, maybe not even as quickly as others, but they would get the job done, surely and competently. This trait helped Charles as he left high school to take a course in mechanical engineering. He had the mechanical aptitude and concentration it took to figure out what made machines tick.

It's doubtful anyone in his hometown would have predicted that Charles Lindbergh would become a flier. In those early days most fliers were still thought of as somewhat eccentric inventors or thrill-seeking adventurers who just couldn't keep their feet on the ground like common folks. But somewhere along the line, Lindbergh fell in love with the idea of flying. He bought a sturdy little plane, the Curtiss "Jenny," and he applied himself with his usual steely determination to learn what needed to be learned. He was lucky too—along with his determination he also had that gift that pilots of his day called "air sense," an almost intuitive feel for flying, for knowing when something is right or wrong with the winds, the weather or the machinery. Lindbergh quickly discovered that he was a natural flier. Soon the world would know it.

One of the greatest prizes in aviation in the mid-1920s was the challenge of flying solo nonstop across the Atlantic. The attraction of a $25,000 prize was accompanied by the knowledge that a half-dozen other pilots had already given it a try and failed, some of them dying in the attempt. Like a mountain waiting to be climbed, or a new land waiting to be discovered, the Atlantic stood as a challenge to be met and overcome.

So Charles A. Lindbergh also decided to attempt the crossing. After getting some financial support from his employer, Major William Robertson, and investing another $2,000 of his own money, he chose a Ryan monoplane, to be built with his own modifications. The plane's engine was built at the Wright Aeronautical Corporation in Paterson, New Jersey. Not the kind of a flier to leave his fate in the hands of others, Lindbergh literally worked, ate and slept at the Ryan shop in San Diego, California while his plane, christened the *Spirit of St. Louis*, was built under his supervision.

What his financial backers saw when he flew into St. Louis, before taking off for New York, was a specially modified Ryan capable of carrying 448 gallons of fuel, 145 more gallons than had ever been lifted by an airplane before. A little disturbing to his backers, though, was the arrangement of the fuel tanks, which left Lindbergh no front view from his enclosed cockpit, forcing him to use his side windows for line-of-sight navigation.

The company founded by Claude Ryan in San Diego in 1921 built this PAT air mail survey monoplane, a forerunner to Charles Lindbergh's Spirit of St. Louis. *United Air Lines*

"Lucky Lindy" (Charles Lindbergh) and his plane, the Spirit of St. Louis. *Because the plane was designed with no windows in the front, Lindbergh had to peer out the side windows to see where he was going.* Smithsonian Institution PHOTO NO. 86-13507

At 7:52 on a cloudy morning on May 20, 1927, Charles Lindbergh took off from Roosevelt Field, Long Island, New York—toward Paris, France and history. The gathered crowd (word had somehow slipped out) suffered a few moments of breathless fear as the *Spirit of St. Louis,* heavy with fuel, struggled to climb into the air, barely clearing a tractor and telegraph wires at the end of the runway. The hushed relief that morning signaled the beginning of a world-wide vigil for the lone flier during his record-making flight. Out of touch with the ground during those long hours, Lindbergh's progress was recorded by ships in the Atlantic below, whose crews and captains had been requested to keep watch for him.

Inside the tiny cabin of the *Spirit of St. Louis,* Charles Lindbergh was as alone during the next hours as any

human can be. Isolated by the ocean below, and buffeted by increasingly bad weather, the tiny plane winged eastward while its pilot, fortified by sandwiches and caffeine, fought not only the elements but a more quiet and insidious danger—the need for sleep. The excitement prior to takeoff had taken its toll on the steel-nerved Lindbergh, and he had managed only three hours' sleep the night before. Now, lulled by fatigue and isolation, lack of sleep was becoming his greatest enemy. Only a brief slip and the tiny plane would be out of control, plunging to the sea just a short distance below. As night approached and blackness blanketed his plane, the threat grew greater. A sudden brightening of the moon helped as the clouds cleared briefly, and so did its glistening on the upper surface of the cloud banks. Just enough, along with his determination and concentration, to keep him awake. And then, suddenly it seemed, there were mountains ahead and the coast of Ireland appeared. A small fishing boat hove into view and he swooped lower. "Is this the way to Ireland?" he shouted out the plane's tiny window. Although they couldn't understand his words, the men in the boat waved back jubilantly. Within a few minutes he was over the cliffs of County Kerry in Ireland and heading toward Cork, then the English Channel and over France. On the ground below the messages raced by radio. Lindbergh had been sighted over land. He was on his way to Paris.

Only hours before, Charles Lindbergh had been unknown to most of the world. Now, approaching Paris, guided by the bright searchlight at Le Bourget Airport, he had become a hero and one of the best-known men in the world. Over 100,000 people were waiting at the airport as his plane touched down, and hundreds of thousands more cheered throughout the world as they received the word. The Atlantic had been crossed by an American, the "Lone Eagle," as he was quickly dubbed, and aviation would never be the same again. Lindbergh had taken 33 hours and 39 minutes to cover the 3,610 miles of his route across the Atlantic. But during those hours the world's attention had been focused as never before on the new era of "flying machines," and, almost overnight, the airplane had found its place in the changing face of the modern world.

5

PIONEERS, PROPELLERS AND PASSENGERS: THE EMERGENCE OF THE MODERN AIRLINES

Suddenly, after the heroic flight of "Lucky Lindy," everybody wanted to fly. In 1929 over 170,000 paying passengers boarded the nation's quickly growing air fleet, nearly three times the 60,000 who had traveled by air the previous year. For the first time, Americans were taking to the air in numbers that surpassed the profitable airlines in Germany, and nearly equaled those of all the other European airlines together. "Flying mania" had hit the nation. In *Plane Crazy*, a Walt Disney cartoon released in 1928, even

In the early 1930s pilots flew passenger aircraft from an outside cockpit, as on this Northrop Alpha plane. Smithsonian Institution PHOTO NO. 1B-28054

Connecting a Hemisphere: The Beginnings of Pan American Airways

When the small airline soon to be known as Pan American Airways won the government contract to fly air mail from Key West, Florida to Havana, Cuba in 1927, it accepted a big load. The U.S. government had a vital interest in cementing and maintaining a good relationship with South American countries. American bankers, who had made many loans to the countries of South America, were also concerned with keeping strong lines of communications open. And the transportation link would benefit American businesses in their competition against German, British and French firms.

Under the guiding hand of Juan Trippe, an entrepreneur who mixed his extensive business connections with a love of aviation, Pan Am representatives began touring the countries of South America. Operating with the double blessing of strong financial backing (thanks to Trippe and his connections) and the moral support and connections of the U.S. government, Pan Am's people began setting up partnerships with many small existing airlines and buying up many others. With this wide base of cooperation and connections established, the company was assured of a strong start.

Officially beginning operations on October 27, 1927, Pan Am was an immediate success. Within a few months it expanded its original fleet of Fokker Trimotors to include the longer range Sikorsky S-38 Flying Boats. Its travel mileage also increased quickly. Starting with a short 110-mile jump, by January 1, 1929 it was covering 261 miles, by March of that same year, 5,275 miles, and by August, 11,075 miles. Within another six months it would add another 4,500 miles to its routes.

Unlike some of the other airlines beginning operations at the same time, Pan Am never saw itself primarily as an air mail service. Covering areas where land transportation was primitive and transportation by sea often undependable, Pan Am enjoyed a successful passenger-carrying business almost from the start. In the first six months of 1929, it flew over 1 million passenger miles and carried over 7,000 people. It also had a big air mail service, delivering 250,000 pounds of mail in that same period with a 99.85% efficiency average.

Cutting travel and mail communication time by 33 ½ hours between Miami and Santiago, Cuba, its expanded routes formed an important link among North, Central and South America. Flying Pan Am, a passenger could reach Panama from Miami in two days rather than the 12 days the journey by boat took. Mail to Chile was delivered in 9 days whereas sea delivery took 20. As the first major air bridge between North and South America, Pan Am was unquestionably a striking success.

Mickey Mouse got into the act as the popular cartoon character mimicked Lindbergh's famous flight.

Wall Street reflected the trend. Suddenly aviation stocks were hot. Tales circulated of immense profits to be made, and many of them were true. One aviation executive, who had cautiously invested $40 in cash in 1926, saw his stock explode in three years to a profit of more than $3 million. A $253 investment by another returned the incredible profit of $35.6 million by the late 1930s. For a brief period even the stock of a small eastern company called the Seaboard Airline saw a bustle of action, until it was discovered that the corporation was actually a struggling railroad!

In the area of general aviation—that is, private airplanes not belonging either to the military or the commercial airlines—over 2,955,530 passengers were recorded as traveling by air annually in the U.S. by 1929. While many of these were friends or families of the pilots who owned the private aircraft, the vast majority of these "general aviation passengers" were businesspeople, chartering the small planes for business trips or flying company planes for business.

A Boeing 80-A transport at Boeing Field, August 1929. The Boeing Company Archives

Spurred by air mail contracts and the Lindbergh flight, new airlines were springing up literally by the dozens. While some with profitable air mail or passenger routes were beginning to expand and show good profits, others barely managed to keep their few planes in repair and flying.

ON WINGS AND RAILS: TAT's HYBRID SOLUTION

One of the more innovative of the new airlines was the Transcontinental Air Transport, or TAT, which started service in July 1929 with Lindbergh (who had no official position in the company) presiding at the opening ceremonies. TAT offered a package deal that wooed the wary traveler.

Despite the sudden public interest in flying, the easiest way to get from one coast to the other in the late 1920s was still by railroad. The fastest train could make the trip in a little over 72 hours. An airplane could make it faster. But no airline was willing to offer regularly scheduled coast-to-coast flights because beating the train time would require night flying, which was still considered a risky operation, especially when paying customers might be involved.

The founders of TAT thought that they had hit upon a solution to the night-flying problem. Enlisting the cooperation of the Pennsylvania and Santa Fe railroads with the promise of mutual profits, TAT organized an elaborate system that spanned the American continent by a combination of rail and air.

Passengers traveling the east-west route (the company also operated west-to-east service) boarded a luxury train, the *Airway Limited*, at Pennsylvania Station in New York and traveled comfortably overnight to Columbus, Ohio. There they would board a plane, flying westward during the daylight hours until nightfall, when they would land in Waynoka, Oklahoma. There they boarded a Pullman train, this time on the Atchison, Topeka and Santa Fe line, to enjoy a hot meal and a safe night's sleep while the train continued moving westward until morning. Then, boarding the plane again in Clovis, New Mexico, they would fly to Los Angeles. The idea was ingenious but expensive. Passengers enjoyed entertainment, hot meals and comfort as well as safe and speedy service, making the journey in 48 hours. But the fare was steep, $350 a person, a staggering price by the standards of the time, and most of the 10-seater planes operated only half filled.

Wiley Post: Around the World in Eight Days

Less than five years after Charles Lindbergh's famous flight, a one-eyed pilot named Wiley Post flew around the world in eight and a half days. His flight dramatically demonstrated how quickly aviation was shrinking the once forbidding distances of the globe.

Post, who was born on a farm near Grand Saline, Texas on November 22, 1899, was a stocky ex-airplane mechanic whom many pilots had called the best in the business before he took to flying airplanes instead of just repairing them. After a stint as a barnstormer and parachute jumper, he secured the financial backing of a Texas oilman, F. C. Hall, who had employed him as a personal pilot for a while, and bought a small Lockheed plane, which he christened the *Winnie Mae*.

Taking off with an assistant, an Australian flier named Harold Gatty, Post began his historic flight on June 23, 1931. With stopovers for sleep and refueling, their route took them first to England, then Germany, Russia, Siberia, the Bering Strait, Alaska, Canada and then back to New York. Upon landing in New York, Post's official time for the journey was eight days, 15 hours and 51 minutes, dramatically beating the previous time of 15 days, 11 hours and 7 minutes set by a group of U.S. Army pilots in 1924.

After the flight Post published the story of his adventures in *Around the World in Eight Days*. Two years later he repeated the flight, this time alone, in seven days, 18 hours and 49 minutes, using the new automatic piloting system that had recently been developed.

In 1935, while making a pleasure flight to the Orient with his close friend, the great American humorist, Will Rogers, Post's plane crashed near Point Barrow, Alaska. Both Rogers and Post were killed instantly.

THE WATRES ACT SETS THE STAGE

Transcontinental Air Transport closed down its train-plane operation after only 16 months. But in 1930 the operation merged with another airline in

By the early 1930s air travel became more comfortable, complete with meals served by hostesses, who, in case of emergency, were also registered nurses. United Air Lines

a move that would form one of the nation's first all-night transcontinental airlines.

The TAT merger didn't come as a surprise to the airline watchers on Wall Street. Thanks in part to the federal government's McNary-Watres Bill (or Watres Act) of 1930, passed by Congress on April 29, mergers and consolidations had suddenly become common in the fledgling airline industry. This bill, engineered by President Hoover's postmaster general, Walter Folger Brown, set up a new system of paying airlines on a space-mile basis for their mail deliveries. Under this new arrangement, the carriers would receive Post Office Department subsidies on the basis of the space they made available for the transportation of mail rather than on the number of pounds they actually carried. The new plan gave a distinct edge to the larger and wealthier corporations that could afford bigger, multi-engined aircraft. Brown had developed the plan in the hopes that he could force the airlines to develop larger aircraft, which would also force them, if they wanted to run profitably, to expand their passenger operations. He reasoned that once developed, such large lines would then become independent of government subsidies, while the smaller lines would continue to operate as mail carriers on the government dole. The immediate result of the Watres Act was to set up a merger mania between large and small companies as everyone struggled for the funds to get a bigger piece of the action.

THE BIG FOUR OF THE AIRWAYS

Wall Street and investors played the odds as money jockeyed for money. By early 1930 *Aviation*, the quasi-official industry publication, estimated that nearly 90% of all the air transport operations in the nation were being carried out by only four major corporate systems.

TAT, for instance, merged with Maddux Air Lines and then joined the pioneering Western Air Express to put together Transcontinental and Western Air Lines (T&WA) in 1930, which would eventually become Trans World Airlines (TWA). Under its new corporate structure TWA would corner the central continental route in the United States, stretching from New York to Los Angeles. Using Ford Trimotor airplanes, TWA inaugurated the first coast-to-coast service exclusively by air, from New York to Los Angeles, on October 25, 1930. The trip included an overnight stop in Kansas City and took a total of 36 hours.

Two other pioneering airlines, Stout Air Services and Varney Air Lines, as well as Pacific Air Transport, became a part of the newly formed Boeing Air Transport, which in turn became a part of United Air Lines in July 1931. United also absorbed National Air Transport.

Meanwhile, Robertson Aircraft Corporation (where Lindbergh had put in his stint as an air mail pilot) and Standard Airlines (which had been running a Los Angeles–Phoenix–Tucson passenger service since 1927) merged with American Airways, which was formed in January 1930. American gained control of the southern transcontinental route, through Nashville and Dallas.

On the East Coast, Pitcairn Aviation, which had been running between New York and Atlanta, added the Florida Airways route from Miami to Atlanta and became Eastern Air Transport in January 1930.

Thus by mid-1931 some 30 small airlines had merged and absorbed each other to form four powerful giants, TWA, United, American and Eastern. And within a few years such other small and pioneering lines as Alaska, Colonial, Interstate, Southern and Universal would also all fall victim to corporate mergers.

Major Events in Air Travel

1927–1933

1927   May 20–21. Charles Lindbergh flies solo across the Atlantic Ocean, between New York and Paris.

1928   June 17–18. Amelia Earhart becomes the first woman to fly (as a passenger) across the Atlantic.

1929   Germany's Graf Zeppelin dirigible makes the first flight by any aircraft across the Pacific Ocean.

1930   April 29. Watres Act changes the terms by which air mail contracts are assigned in the United States, encouraging large aircraft and resulting in mergers in the airline industry.

1931   June 23. Wiley Post, with copilot Harold Gatty, begins flight around the world in 8½ days.

1932   May 20–21. Amelia Earhart is the first woman to fly alone across the Atlantic, flying from Newfoundland to Ireland, a distance of 2,026 miles, in just under 15 hours.

Amelia Earhart: The Flyer Who Vanished

She was tall, lean and good-looking, and, like Charles Lindbergh, she inspired a wide and loyal following in the late 1920s and early 1930s. Born on July 24, 1898 in Atchison, Kansas, Amelia Earhart, like Lindbergh, cut her own path through life. Strong minded and independent, she worked in Canada as an army nurse during World War I, attended Columbia University and the University of Southern California, and worked as a social worker in Boston, Massachusetts. Her first love, though, was flying, which she learned in 1920 at the age of 22. In 1928, flying as a passenger (although she was herself a capable pilot), she became the first woman to fly across the Atlantic. Four years later, in 1932, she topped that, flying the same route solo, the first woman to achieve this feat. She also broke the speed record for the flight, which she completed in 14 hours and 56 minutes.

In 1928 Earhart became the aviation editor of *Cosmopolitan Magazine*. Her two books, *20 hours, 40 minutes*, published in 1928, and *The Fun of It*, published in 1932, added immensely to her reputation as an intelligent, dedicated and disciplined flier who could compete with the best. Throughout the early 1930s she continued to set numerous altitude and speed records, as well as proving herself a thoughtful advocate of feminist causes.

In 1935, flying a twin-motored, 10-passenger Lockheed Vega supplied to her by Purdue University, where she was a visiting faculty member, she became the first pilot to fly solo between Honolulu, Hawaii and the U.S. mainland as well as the first to fly non-stop between Mexico City and New York.

Earhart's career came to an abrupt and tragic end, however. In 1937, while attempting an around-the-world flight with her copilot, Frederick J. Noonan, she disappeared somewhere between New Guinea and Howland Island in the Pacific. They had already completed 22,000 miles of the trip when they vanished, Earhart's last recorded words, uttered via radio, still echoing: "Gas is running low; we are circling but cannot see land." Despite a massive search, no trace of Amelia Earhart, her copilot, or her plane was ever found, and the exact circumstances of her disappearance remain a mystery.

Amelia Earhart, pioneer pilot. Smithsonian Institution
PHOTO NO. 87-15303

Critics called the process a disastrous defeat to free choice for the American public, a sudden collapse of what had promised to be a booming and varied independent transportation system into less than half a dozen powerful corporations. But supporters of the mergers were quick to point out that the public now had stability and order, whereas before the consolidations, airline routes had been haphazard, irregular and possibly unsafe.

Meanwhile, the worst financial depression in the nation's history also began to take its toll on the small, struggling airlines during the 1930s, as the four domestic giants grew stronger. What shape the airline industry might have taken in the United States without the Watres Act is impossible to know. But, despite the loss of many (though not all) small independents during the shakeout and depression, the nation's newest transportation system managed to survive and even grow—from 92,880 passenger miles in 1930 to 754,748 passenger miles at the end of the decade in 1939.

The airlines, it appeared, were here to stay.

Historical Headlines

1929–1933

1929   Stock market crashes in October; the crash is the forerunner to the Great Depression the following year.

Canalization of the Ohio River is completed.

1930   The economy sags drastically, unemployment approaches 4 million and the period known as the Great Depression begins.

1933   Congress enacts a broad program of measures designed to bring economic relief and an end to the depression.

6

AMERICA TAKES TO THE AIR: GROWTH IN THE 1930s AND 1940s

While the business end of America's newest transportation system, aviation, was expanding, consolidating and building its air networks during the 1930s and early 1940s, major changes were also taking place in the designs and operation of the aircraft.

BUILDING BIGGER, BETTER AND SAFER

Someone once described aeronautical engineers as people "who must build for one pound of weight what any fool could do for two." With the demand for larger, safer, faster and more powerful aircraft increasing as the airlines' business grew, the major aircraft builders and operators struggled to meet those demands. Much research and experimentation was also being done by independent aircraft builders who had resisted being swallowed up by the major airline mergers. These included builders of large aircraft such as Donald Douglas on the West Coast and Leroy Grumman on the East, as well as Clyde Cessna, and others like him, who had decided to specialize in the smaller planes used for general aviation.

At the Douglas Aircraft factory sandbags were piled on the wing of the DC-1 to test its ability to withstand stress, June 29, 1933. Douglas Aircraft Company

By the late 1930s monoplanes, with their single wing, began to replace the old biplanes, and the open cockpits that took so great a toll on the early air mail fliers were now enclosed. Gone, too, for the most part was the lightweight wood and fabric structure of the body and wings, replaced by newer and stronger light-metal construction.

Among the most important additions to the planes of the late 1930s and early 1940s were the first radio navigation systems. While various systems were used for short overseas flights, the domestic airlines that traveled the continental United States began using special "radio range receivers." Unsophisticated by today's standards, these were basically just large, bulky radios equipped with earphones and designed to pick up signals from a network of transmitting stations constructed along the major air routes. As long as a pilot stayed on course, the only sound to be heard was a steady and somewhat monotonous humming. But if the plane drifted off course in one direction, the pilot

would suddenly hear a frantic "dit-dah" (the Morse code letter A). If the plane was drifting in the opposite direction, the pilot would hear a "dah-dit" (the Morse code letter N). It was a crude arrangement, but now at least pilots could fly for longer distances above the clouds, or through fog, and still remain on course. These improvements in radio navigation systems enabled the airlines to fly at night, and they were now able to compete with the timetables of the cross-country railroads.

Major changes were also taking place in the business of manufacturing aircraft in the mid-1930s. Earlier airline operators and aircraft manufacturers had enjoyed close corporate ties, with the same corporations often building and operating the airplanes. Boeing, for instance, on the West Coast, had become a profitable manufacturer of airplanes and part of the United Air Lines corporation. Such corporate ties, plus the lucrative government contracts and air routes enjoyed by the "big four"—United, American, Eastern, and Transcontinental and Western Airlines (TWA)—had created very powerful corporations. And that made many people uneasy.

The situation changed suddenly and dramatically, though, when a scandal involving the air mail contracts hit the Postmaster General's office in 1934. The air mail contractors, critics maintained, were no more than government-sponsored monopolists. In a hasty reaction, the government cancelled all its mail contracts with private industry and returned the business of flying the mail to the U.S. Army. The decision was an unwise and disastrous one. Although the military pilots were competent, they were untrained in the mail routes and were operating inferior equipment. In the first week after the army's takeover of the mail routes, five pilots were killed in crashes and six others were seriously injured.

The public was horrified. After only three weeks of the miscalculated experiment, the order was given to return the air mail contracts to private industry.

The new conditions of the Air Mail Act of 1934 were labyrinthine and strict, however. And they forced airline operators and the aircraft builders to break their corporate connections. The up-and-coming Boeing was forced to sever its connection with United, while other aircraft builders also had to break their connections with TWA and other airline operators.

The depression, which began with the stock market crash in 1929, had already taken its toll on many small aircraft builders. Even the more financially stable

Inside a Douglas DC-3 cockpit. Douglas Aircraft Company

The Brief Day of the Dirigible

Despite the quest for powered and controlled heavier-than-air machines, the idea of passenger-carrying lighter-than-air craft remained very much alive well into the 20th century. While Americans showed little interest in lighter-than-air craft, Germany had continued its research into the capabilities of bigger and better "balloons." The result was a series of dirigibles that by 1910 actually gave Germany the world's first commercial airline—though not in the sense that we usually think of it.

Designed by German Count Ferdinand von Zeppelin as a military vehicle, the first Zeppelin dirigible, a rigid airship with a metal framework, made its debut on July 2, 1900. Within a decade a fleet of five Zeppelins had been built, and by 1909 the world's first airline, known as Delag, was founded. Although Delag did not run scheduled flights at first, by the beginning of World War I the Zeppelin airships had carried a total of nearly 35,000 passengers and crew members over 107,000 miles, between Lake Constance, Berlin and other German cities. During World War I German Zeppelins were used for bombing raids over England, but after the war, in the 1920s and 1930s, two other gigantic ships, the *Graf Zeppelin* and the *Hindenburg*, were put into commercial passenger service.

The *Graf Zeppelin* made its first flight in 1928. It was a 774-foot-long rigid airship that carried its passengers in a compartment under the hydrogen-filled balloon. The *Graf Zeppelin* made over 590 flights, 140 of them across the Atlantic, traveling more than a million miles during its lifetime and carrying a total of 13,100 passengers. In 1929 it made the first flight by any aircraft across the Pacific Ocean.

The larger *Hindenburg* (804 feet long and 134.5 feet in diameter) was much more luxurious. It boasted several passenger decks, a large dining room, a smoking room (despite the dangers of igniting the explosive hydrogen gas with which the balloon was filled) and a full-size band playing for the passengers' entertainment.

On May 6, 1937 the *Hindenburg* was carrying 97 passengers and crew members. It had crossed the Atlantic and was about to land at the airport in Lakehurst, New Jersey when it it burst into flame. Within 34 seconds the flaming giant had crashed to earth. Thirty-six people, including the captain, were killed. The dramatic "as-it-was-happening" description of an on-the-spot radio announcer added a terrifying depth to the horror. For all practical purposes the brief age of the commercial passenger-flying dirigible was over.

---

motor companies, such as Ford, were forced to drop their aircraft divisions. Now the Air Mail Act of 1934 left the way open for the three major builders—Boeing, Douglas and Lockheed—to compete for the business of the emerging big four commercial airline operators.

At the same time, the new business climate led indirectly to the birth of the first truly successful American commercial aircraft, the first of the modern airliners.

THE BOEING 247 AND THE DOUGLAS DC-3

In the early 1930s, a squat, homely biplane built by the Curtiss Company for American Airlines and called the Condor dominated passenger travel. Powered by a relatively strong nine-cylinder Wright Cyclone engine, the Condor was the first to have a retractable undercarriage. The original model, introduced in December 1930, had 18 wicker seats. Now that night flying had become safe, the T-32 model was introduced, featuring sleeping berth accommodations for 12 passengers. As a result, the Condor had the edge over other planes on the long transcontinental routes.

With long-distance operation becoming more important to all the major airlines, the Boeing Company desperately needed a new design to compete with the Curtiss Condor. The result, the Boeing 247, built under contract for United Airlines, was designed to meet

United's needs for its coast-to-coast mail contract. Making its first flight on February 8, 1933, the Boeing 247 might in some ways be considered the first of the modern airliners—with its all-metal construction and faster cruising speed of nearly 160 miles an hour, it could fly the coast-to-coast run in a little less than 20 hours. However, fitted with underpowered engines (United decided to economize), the Boeing 247 could carry only 10 passengers.

Still, it could compete with the Condor. United immediately ordered 60 of the new Boeing planes at the then staggering total cost of $4 million. As a result, the Boeing factory in Seattle suddenly had its hands full.

So, when TWA and American (also seeking to replace the Condor with a more modern airplane) started looking for a new and better plane, they turned to the inventive Douglas Aircraft Company in California.

Donald Douglas's prototype model, the DC-1, made its first flight on July 1, 1933. TWA ordered 20 of an improved model, the DC-2, which soon followed.

By May TWA had received delivery on its first DC-2s, with a cruising speed of up to 196 mph and a range of nearly 1,000 miles.

Douglas's popular DC-2 had already proved its worth in speed, economy and durability when American Airlines challenged the company to build a "sleeper" to compete on overnight and long-distance routes. The Douglas solution was to upgrade and redesign the DC-2. The redesign, known as the DC-3, corrected some minor annoyances in its predecessor, but its most important feature was the widened fuselage to allow more space for berths. This change had an even greater impact than was initially imagined. The first DC-3 to go into commercial service was a 14-passenger luxury sleeper transport. Its lower berths converted to large, comfortable and adjustable seats for day travel, and its upper berths conveniently folded up into the ceiling. Further luxury came with the addition of two dressing rooms and toilets located in the rear of the cabin. A galley at the forward end of the aircraft made it possible to provide passengers with hot meals en route. The early planes even featured a completely enclosed "honeymoon compart-

With only two months to go before its maiden flight in May 1934, the DC-2 still didn't have any wings. Douglas Aircraft Company

The DC-2, wings in place, flies over Kansas City, May 13, 1934. Douglas Aircraft Company

ment." In the railroad-oriented thinking of the time, the airlines now had what amounted to the first "flying Pullman car."

The DC-3 made its first commercial flight on the nonstop New York to Chicago route in July 1936. And from that time until well into the 1980s, it reigned as a favorite among pilots and passengers in military and commercial transport around the world. As one pilot once wrote to Douglas, "If ever an inanimate object earned, deserved and received the love of man, your DC-3 was that object."

Although the air fare was expensive for the average customer, the plane was fast, well built and economical to operate. It was an immediate success. It would prove even more so when Douglas, confident in the DC-3's competitiveness, almost immediately followed up with a day coach version of the same aircraft:

The Douglas engineers were quick to realize that their beautifully engineered plane could also handle greater day passenger loads thanks to its widened fuselage. They removed the berths, increasing the plane's

seating capacity by 50 to 100%, depending on the individual seating configurations.

The DC-3 had not only captured most of the long-distance "sleeper" market, but this new design now gave the airlines, for the first time, an airplane with a large

Inside the DC-3. Douglas Aircraft Company

Pacific Northern Airlines service to Alaska. Douglas Aircraft Company

enough capacity finally to make money just by transporting people.

It was exactly what the airline companies needed at the time. And Douglas was suitably rewarded with a slew of contracts. From the introduction of the DC-3 in 1936, until the start of World War II in 1939, air travel in the United States increased up to 500%. And the Douglas DC-2s and DC-3s carried nearly 90% of all the new traffic.

But the DC-3's story didn't end there. Converted into the C-47 cargo plane during the years of the World War II, the DC-3 continued its exemplary career of trustworthy service.

Of the nearly 11,000 DC-3s produced over a 10-year period from 1936 to 1946, over 2,000 were still operating in various civilian and military transportation systems around the world as late as 1985. The DC-3 was truly a plane that lived up to the words of a C-47

Berths made up for night travel aboard the DC-3 Douglas Sleeper Transport. Douglas Aircraft Company

A DC-3 coming off the assembly line at Douglas Aircraft in Santa Monica, California. Dougas Aircraft Company

---

Historical Headlines

1934–1940

1934   The Federal Communications Commission (FCC) begins regulation of all national and international telephone, radio and cable communications.

President Franklin Roosevelt establishes his "Good Neighbor Policy" with South American countries, opposing armed intervention by any foreign power.

1935   The U.S. government sets up the Soil Conservation Service to try to stop soil erosion in the drought-stricken Great Plains of the Midwest, which had become a "dust bowl."

1936   Many Americans go to Spain to fight in the Spanish Civil War with the Loyalists against the Fascists.

1937   The dirigible *Hindenburg* bursts into flames near its mooring at Lakehurst, New Jersey. Many of its passengers and crew die in the accident.

The Golden Gate Bridge in San Francisco is completed.

1939   Germany invades Poland and World War II begins, although the United States has not yet entered the war.

The Bronx-Whitestone Bridge, on Long Island Sound, is completed.

First televised baseball game.

1940   Completion and, four months later, the collapse of the Tacoma- Narrows Bridge ("Galloping Gertie").

---

military pilot, who wrote "You could wreck one, but you couldn't wear it out."

In both peace and war, the Douglas DC-3 became a plane that could not only pay its own way but be trusted. And in the days after World War II it helped move America into the golden era of commercial aviation.

7

BIGGER, BETTER AND FASTER: WORLD WAR II AND POSTWAR GROWTH, 1938–1959

The next two decades—from 1938 to 1959—would see some of the most dramatic developments yet in the saga of U.S. airways. Legislation would transform the industry and force it to mature. World war would place unprecedented demands and challenges on both airlines and aircraft manufacturers. And the entire industry would be transformed by innovations in engine power and aircraft design.

REGULATION FOR AN EXPANDING INDUSTRY

Four years after passage of the Air Mail Act of 1934, the federal government took its biggest step yet toward shaping the future of the U.S. airline industry. The Civil Aeronautics Act of 1938 founded a new board, the Civil Aeronautics Authority (CAA, later called the Civil Aeronautics Board or CAB), to govern the rapidly growing airlines. Its five members and chairman were given several important powers, including the responsibility for setting rates for all carriers that crossed state lines. The new CAA's responsibilities included licensing of pilots, establishment of rules of flight, assigning airways and setting standards for equipment. Those airlines that had survived the 1934 reorganization, for the most part, became the "Trunk Carriers" or "Domestic Trunks" in

1938 and retained their routes. "International and Territorial Carriers," such as Pan Am, were regulated separately, and other categories, such as "All-Cargo Carriers" (no passengers and no mail) were opened up later. Pilots in particular enjoyed a protected status in the new legislation, to the delight of the pilots' union, the ALPA (Air Line Pilots Association). As Representative John Martin of Colorado explained in support of the bill:

> In my opinion, the piloting of these great airplanes, which hurtle through the air at 200 miles per hour, loaded with human lives, is the most responsible, the most skillful, and the most dangerous occupation that mankind ever engaged in. If there is anything we can put in the legislation that will keep worry from the air pilots, it ought to be done.

The 1938 legislation set the stage for airline regulation in the United States over the next 40 years, but other factors were also at work that would have equally important effects.

RISING TO THE CHALLENGE

On September 1, 1939 Germany invaded Poland. Britain and France then declared war on Germany and World War II was under way. With the advent of

During World War II Douglas retooled the DC-3 as the C-47 (above), dubbed the "Gooney Bird."   It   came off the assembly lines in droves (below). Douglas Aircraft Company

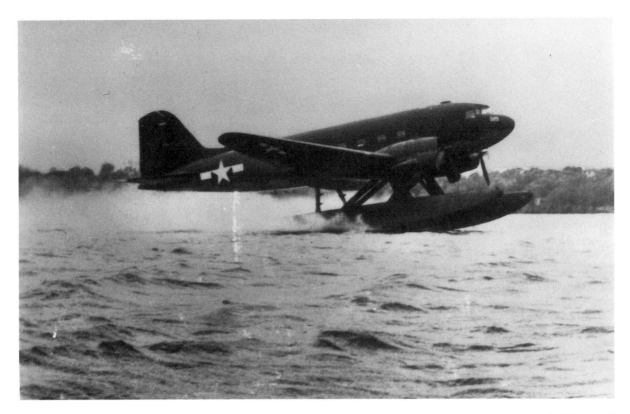

The DC-3 doubled as an amphibious plane called the "Duck" (above), and carried thousands of personnel (below) and tons of cargo across the country and across the ocean. Douglas Aircraft Company

Major Facts in Air Travel

1938–1959

1938	June 23. The Civil Aeronautics Act of 1938, enacted by Congress, sets up a federal Civil Aeronautics Authority to regulate interstate airline commerce.
1939	August 27. The first aircraft solely powered by a jet takes off at Merienehe, Germany.
1947	October 14. Charles "Chuck" Yeager, a major in the U.S. Air Force, makes the first flight faster than sound, breaking the "sound barrier."
1949	July 27. The British de Havilland DH106 Comet 1 becomes the world's first jetliner.
1953	Jacqueline Cochran becomes the first woman to break the sound barrier.
1954	January 10. A de Havilland Comet jetliner breaks up over the Mediterranean, killing all aboard.
	April 8. A second Comet disintegrates over the Mediterranean, and Comets are grounded pending investigation and redesign.
	July 15. First flight of a Boeing 707 jetliner.
1956	June 30. Two airliners collide over the Grand Canyon in Arizona in the first major air disaster. Total deaths: 128.
1958	May 30. First flight of a prototype Douglas DC-8, the first Douglas jetliner.

---

war, aircraft manufacturers throughout the world suddenly had a new and urgent focus: to develop bigger, faster and more maneuverable airplanes. The U.S. industry was no exception.

Before the war, the last aircraft to enter passenger service was the Boeing 307 Stratoliner. Modeled after Boeing's B-17 Flying Fortress bomber (Boeing flew a prototype of that plane in 1935), the Stratoliner made its first flight in 1940. The new airliner was different from all its predecessors: Its cabin was pressurized. This meant that for the first time higher altitudes could be reached (and so the name Stratoliner, from "stratosphere"). The Stratoliner cruised at 220 mph, and when TWA inaugurated the aircraft on its transcontinental route on July 8, 1940, it made the trip in just 13 hours 40 minutes, eastbound. "Broader Wings Now Span the Nation" boasted the TWA ad campaign featuring the new plane. The four-engined monoplane carried 33 passengers and a five-member crew. TWA had three, Pan American took five for its flights to South America out of Miami, and multimillionaire aviator Howard Hughes took one modified model. All, however, were pressed into war service as transports by the end of the following year, with TWA's fleet operating over the North Atlantic.

The B-17 bomber, of course, saw action immediately once the United States entered the war in December 1941 (after the bombing of the U.S. naval base at Pearl Harbor). Boeing stepped up production of several different models. The first prototype of the huge Boeing B-29 Superfortress flew in 1942. Three other aircraft manufacturers—Consolidated, North American and Martin—all came out with bombers between 1939 and 1940.

Fighter planes, which had to be lighter and much more maneuverable than civil airliners, did not benefit much from commercial airliner technology, but cargo and troop transport was another matter. Once the United States entered the war, the Army Air Corps supplied the entire transport fleet of Britain's Royal Air Force. By the end of the war Douglas Aircraft had produced more than 10,000 DC-3s, most in the military form, C-47s, for use in the war. During the war much of the emphasis in aircraft design was on the development of the piston engine to power big transports.

The C-47 also flew medical missions, carrying the wounded to hospitals or home. Douglas Aircraft Company

Crews of several U.S. commercial airlines participated in an amazing war effort known as "the Hump." With crews from the U.S. Air Transport Command and China National Aviation Corporation, they ran a supply route into China, over the mountains from India. Often with takeoffs made every two minutes, they made some 5,000 flights in one month. Between 1942 and 1945, they carried more than 44,000 tons of supplies into China, using DC-3s, Consolidated C-87 Liberator transports and Curtiss C-46 Commandos.

The civil airlines in the United States, meanwhile, continued to grow throughout the war. And immedi-

C-47s ready for takeoff for the Berlin airlift in 1948. Douglas Aircraft Company

Jacqueline Cochran:
The First Woman to Break the Sound Barrier

America's second most famous woman aviator, Jacqueline Cochran, was born around 1910 in Pensacola, Florida and grew up in poverty in a foster home in Georgia. At eight she was working in a cotton mill, at a salary of six cents an hour. Later trained as a beautician, she found work in that field in Montgomery, Alabama and in Pensacola and New York.

Possessing a strong character, determination and an adventurous spirit, Cochran took her first flying lessons in 1932 and later studied with a navy pilot who was also a friend. In 1934 she began managing a cosmetics firm that quickly became both popular and profitable. Combining business with flying, she was soon on the air racing circuit. In 1935 she was the first woman to enter the Bendix Transcontinental Air Race. In 1937 she came in third in the race. And in 1938 she won it.

Determined to do her part during the war years, in 1941 she flew a bomber to England, and there became a flight captain in the British Air Transport Auxiliary, training women for air transport service.

Returning to the United States after the war, she initiated a similar program for the Army Air Forces.

Toward the end of war, she also worked as a Pacific and European correspondent for *Liberty Magazine.*

In 1945 she was the first woman civilian to be awarded the Distinguished Service Medal, and in 1948 she was commissioned a lieutenant colonel in the Air Force Reserve.

There were new records to be made, though, and new planes with which to score them. In 1953, after learning to fly a jet, she became the first woman to break the sound barrier. That same year she set world speed records for the 15-, 100- and 500-kilometer courses. In 1961 she set an altitude record of 55,230 feet, and in 1964 she set the standing women's world speed record of 1,429 miles per hour flying a F-104G Super Star jet.

---

ately after the war ended in 1945, the airlines were able to introduce several new, exciting aircraft: the Douglas DC-4, the Lockheed Constellation and, by 1949, the Boeing Stratocruiser.

THE DAWN OF THE JET AGE

Just five days before the German invasion of Poland, another event, equally important to the development of aircraft worldwide, took place at Merienehe, Germany. The first aircraft powered solely by jet engines took off from the airfield of the Heinkel factory. While jets were used on the German side late in the war (especially the Messerschmitt 262), only one Allied jet fighter flew during the war, the British Gloster Meteor. The stage was set, however, for the important new developments the jet engine would later bring to transportation by air.

The same engine that powered Britain's Gloster Meteor traveled to the United States and was used to power the Bell Airacomet, a fighter jet that never was actually used during World War II. But its engine became the basis for all jet engine development in the United States. Initially, however, engine designers thought of the jet, which in its early models consumed huge amounts of fuel, as strictly a high-performance aircraft engine. That is, they believed it was suitable for use only on fighter planes and other military craft that could justify the high fuel consumption.

The British, still at the forefront of jet plane development, were first by far to develop a jet airliner. The de Havilland Comet made its debut flight on July 27, 1949, more than five years ahead of any competitor. It could carry 36 passengers and flew at a speed of 490 mph—an increase of nearly one-third over the Boeing Stratocruiser. The Comet's range was 2,600 miles, and its sleek, aerodynamically efficient profile made it the most talked about plane of its day. By 1952 de Havilland announced an upgrade, the Comet 3, that could carry 78 passengers and could fly 60% farther without

Airports and passsenger airliners had changed dramatically by the 1950s. Douglas Aircraft Company

refueling. The orders poured in, even from many world airlines, including Pan American. Orders for

A DC-6A loading cargo in the 1950s. Douglas Aircraft Company

more than 100 Comets were placed by the end of 1953.

Then the unthinkable happened. On January 10, 1954 a Comet 1 flying for BOAC (British Overseas Air Corportation) broke up in midflight and crashed into the Mediterranean Sea off the island of Elba. No one survived. Then three months later another Comet also fell apart in midair over the Mediterranean. The Comets were grounded immediately, divers were sent to retrieve the pieces and an investigation ensued. A design flaw was discovered in the windows on both sides of the cabin section of the fuselage. De Havilland set about immediately to correct the flaw, but the redesign would take four years, and the British five-year lead in jet air transport came to an abrupt end.

Both Boeing and Douglas, meanwhile, had been struggling to close the gap. Since the spring of 1950, Boeing had been looking at a jet powered replacement for its Model 377 Stratocruiser. The result was the Boeing 707, a big, clean-lined aircraft with four jet engines mounted on pods at the front or leading edge of the wings. It made its first flight on July 15, 1954—after the Comet 1 was withdrawn from service. Unlike the Comet, the 707's wings swept back at a 35-degree angle, making use of design advances from the B-47 Stratojet and B-52 Stratofortress jet bombers devel-

---

Historical Headlines

1940–1959

1941   The United States declares war on Japan and enters World War II.

Scientists begin work on the Manhattan Project, development of the atomic bomb.

1944   Franklin Delano Roosevelt is reelected president for a fourth term.

1945   Roosevelt dies and Harry S Truman, his vice president, becomes president.

Adolf Hitler commits suicide and Germany surrenders on May 7.

The United States drops an atomic bomb on Hiroshima, Japan. More than 135,000 deaths and injuries result. The United States drops a second bomb on Nagasaki, and Japan surrenders on August 14.

U.S. troops enter Korea south of the 38th parallel, replacing the Japanese.

1950   The new Tacoma-Narrows Bridge (replacing "Galloping Gertie") is completed.

The United States recognizes the new country of Vietnam and sends military advisers to teach the use of weapons.

1951   The Delaware Memorial Bridge across the Delaware River connects New Jersey and Delaware, with a total length of 3.5 miles.

First transcontinental television broadcast in the United States.

1955   The Tappan Zee Bridge is finished across the Hudson River at Tarrytown, New York.

1957   The Mackinac Bridge is completed across the Mackinac Straits in Michigan.

Soviets launch the first artificial satellite, called *Sputnik.*

---

oped by Boeing after the war. Once again the airlines profited from military technology—with Pan Am placing the first order. The first plane—with seating for 179 passengers and a cruising speed of 570 mph—was delivered in October 1958. Boeing quickly developed the 707 into a family of planes with similar basic design but different lengths and weights for use with various types of cargos and airports. It also modified a version to travel shorter distances (short to medium range).

Douglas, meanwhile, was not far behind. Its Douglas DC-8 made its first flight on May 30, 1958 and was delivered to United Air Lines a little over a year later, on June 3, 1959. The DC-8 came in several versions to carry freight or passengers or a combination. It looked a lot like the 707 and was directly competitive with it, carrying as many as 177 passengers and cruising at a speed of 571 mph. Other versions of the DC-8 continued to come out throughout the 1960s and 1970s. Several retrofitted versions also came out in the early 1980s, with passenger capacity from 117 to 259 and a cruising speed as high as 585 mph.

The jet age had truly arrived.

8

SPEED AND SIZE TAKE OFF: JETS AND JUMBO JETS IN THE 1960s

EXTENDING THE JET FLEETS

With the introduction of the Boeing 707 and the Douglas DC-8 in 1958 and 1959, the popularity of jet travel began to take off. The four-engine propeller-driven planes of the late 1940s and 1950s had introduced an element of luxury and spaciousness into air travel that had not existed in the tiny craft of the 1930s and the surplus planes of the 1940s. Now, with jet travel, the airlines packed the passengers in to help finance the more expensive aircraft, and so passenger travel once again became more cramped. But the jet engine increased speed dramatically—an especially important factor in attracting business travel.

Douglas's four-propeller DC-6, introduced into service in 1947, had traveled at a speed of 308 mph with a range of 2,600 nautical miles (the DC-7, which came out in 1953, was scarcely any faster, at 334 mph). The new jet DC-8 nearly doubled their speed and range, traveling 571 mph as far as 4,150 nautical miles with-

A Boeing 727 jet. Boeing

Air Facts

THE 1960s

1960   December 20. The long-range Douglas DC-8 Series 50, which can fly 7,544 miles without refueling, makes its first flight.

1964   Boeing makes delivery on the Model 727, a medium-range jet, first flown by United Airlines and Eastern Airlines.

1965   The Douglas DC-9 (Series 10) short-range jet enters service, 104 feet long, with a range of 1,566 miles.

            Boeing decides to build the short-range 737.

1966   The McDonnell Corporation bails out the overcommitted Douglas Aircraft Company.

            Anticipating the introduction of the Boeing 737, McDonnell Douglas stretches the short-range DC-9 to larger capacity—119 feet (Series 30).

            The big DC-8 Super 61 (187 feet long) makes its first flight, followed by the DC-8 Super 62. They offer long-range flight (7,733 miles for the Super 62) and big capacity (up to 259 passengers for the Super 61).

1967   The DC-8 Super 63 (150 feet long) enters service. It has the fastest speed of the DC-8 series (585 mph).

            The DC-9 short-range jet keeps stretching with a new model, Series 40, 125 feet long.

            April. The Boeing 737, a medium-range jet, begins service, flying first for Eastern Airlines. A stretched version, the 737-200, with a capacity of up to 113 passengers, a 2,000-mile range and a speed of 573 mph, makes its first flight in August.

1968   The DC-9, Series 20, the same size as the original DC-9 Series 10, extends the range of the smaller jet to 5,077 miles.

1969   August. The giant Boeing 747, the first of the "jumbo jets," with a capacity of up to 490 passengers, a range of 4,600 miles and a high cruising speed of Mach 0.89, makes its first flight. Initial orders number 183.

out refueling. Pan Am's transatlantic flight time was cut dramatically by the Boeing 707, which traveled at 600 mph. And, after delivery in 1959 of the 707 that came to be dubbed Air Force One, U.S. President Dwight Eisenhower was able to increase his yearly flight average to 78,677 miles in 193 hours of flying time—a 262% increase in distance covered compared to his previous yearly average of 30,000 miles with only a 62% increase in flight time.

The size of the United States seemed suddenly to shrink and far-flung corners of the world, including Europe, the Middle East and India, became much more

easily reached, both for passenger and cargo transport.

The popularity of jet travel and transport and the increase in traffic in turn encouraged a tremendous upsurge in aircraft design and manufacture, with Boeing this time in the lead and Douglas scrambling hard to catch up. Douglas had brought out the DC-8 without so much as a prototype. Only a year elapsed between its first flight and the day the first plane arrived at United Air Lines for duty. Nearly a dozen versions of the DC-8 followed between 1959 and 1968, and Douglas brought out a second jetliner, the DC-9

(Top:) Air mail cargo has changed a lot since 1929, when cargo carts were used to haul mail and express to be loaded on the Boeing 80-A. (Bottom:) Large cargo containers are readied here for loading into the huge Boeing 747. Boeing

in 1965. Boeing, in the meantime, had noted the need for a short- to medium-range jetliner and set to work on the Model 727.

EXTENDING THE JET FLEETS

Boeing began designing its model 727 design in 1959, and the new medium-range jet, which could carry 131 passengers, made its first flight on February 9, 1963. Both Eastern and United Air Lines were standing in line as the first customers. But at the time the plane went into production, Boeing considered the venture a major risk. No one had ever built a commercial jetliner with only three engines. No one had ever mounted jet engines on the tail before. No one really knew how much market there would be for a jet this size that could land on runways as short as 5,000 feet. And much more of the company's own capital was at risk than before.

During the development of the 707, Boeing had several military contracts in hand—for development of the B-47 and the B-52 and for a fast tanker for air-to-air refueling of those jets. Many elements—from design features and production techniques down to the tool dies—were transferred for production of the 707. But with the 727, Boeing was farther out on a limb. The gamble was one that paid off, though. Between 1964 and 1983 the company built 1,831—making the 727 the most popular jet transport up to that time.

For the 727, Boeing modified the fuselage of the 707 and used a T-tail (with the horizontal tail surfaces, or tailplane, high on the tail, like a T). In addition to its range, the wing design contributed most to the jet's popularity. The swept wings of a jet plane offer low drag and provide great efficiency at high speeds. But at lower speeds, especially at landing and takeoff, the wings usually offer very poor lifting capabilities. Engineers compensate for this design handicap by adding movable flaps at the back or trailing edge, huge hinged pieces that can be adjusted by the pilot or automatically to provide variations in lift or drag. (To a passenger looking out from inside the cabin, these flaps sometimes make the wing look like it's coming apart or falling off during flight.) On the Boeing 727, the designers put all three engines at the rear of the plane, leaving the wings free and uncluttered. They also added slotted flaps at the trailing edge of the wings, plus slats or louvers on the leading, or forward edge, making for excellent performance on takeoff.

Douglas Aircraft, meanwhile, had noticed a growing market for a short-range jet and brought out its first version of the DC-9 in 1964. Like the Boeing 727, it had a high T-tail, but it had only two jet engines instead of the 727's three, and it was small, carrying only 70 passengers. The DC-9 became so popular, however, that orders quickly outstripped Douglas Aircraft's ability to fill them, and the company was threatened by lawsuits for nondelivery. The McDonnell Corporation came to the rescue by buying Douglas in 1966, and the McDonnell Douglas Corporation's Douglas Aircraft Company remains one of the top aircraft manufacturers in the world today. Early on, McDonnell Douglas made the DC-9 available in several sizes: The original 1965 version was 104 feet long and carried only 70 passengers. The stretched DC-9-50 came out in 1974 and was 133 feet long and carried 139 passengers. The most recent version, the DC-9-80 (or MD-80 Series) can carry 179 passengers and is 148 feet long. The first, called the MD-81, flew in 1979. In 1965, Boeing decided to build yet another short-haul jet, the Model 737. The company began development on this new jet with only two sales prospects, Eastern and Lufthansa of Germany. Lufthansa ordered 20, but Eastern decided to buy Douglas DC-9s instead. Boeing kept its commitment to Lufthansa, risking over a billion dollars. The first plane flew in 1967. The risk paid off. By 1990, Boeing had sold nearly 3,000 737s, making it the best-selling commercial airliner in history. And Boeing had become independent of U.S. airlines as its primary market.

JUMBO JETS DEBUT

The most giant aircraft success story by far is the Boeing 747 jumbo jet. Its wide body and enormous capacity were Boeing's answer to the rapidly increasing traffic at airports, not only throughout the United States by the mid-1960s but throughout the world.

From nose to tail, the 747 is, unquestionably, mammoth. The tip of the tail fin extends 63 feet above the ground—the equivalent of a six-story building. Its main undercarriage has 16 wheels to distribute the 747's great weight over the pavement when it is on the ground. Its fuselage is 225 feet long, dotted with dozens of windows and large enough to carry a crew and more than 500 passengers. The tailplane alone of the 747 is 72 feet 9 inches, greater than the wing span of many airliners! And the giant is also fast—traveling at speeds of up to 600 mph.

The Boeing 747. Boeing

Douglas's closest approximations to the 747 are stretched versions of the DC-8, retrofitted DC-8s (first flown in 1981 and seating up to 259), and the DC-10, which has become a standby of airlines throughout the country. The DC-10, first flown on August 29, 1970, entered the fleets of American Airlines and United Air Lines in 1971. It can carry up to 380 passengers and cruises at 587 mph.

As the 1960s drew to a close, Boeing Aircraft was already emerging as the leading aircraft manufacturer— with more models, higher sales, and airliners with greater capacity. Douglas, still strong, continued to

Size of the DC-3 compared with the DC-10. Douglas Aircraft Company.

bring out competitive models, with specialized types to fit the varying circumstances that the airlines were now trying to serve. By this time, these two firms were the most powerful U.S. commercial aircraft manufacturers. Their production and expertise were key ingredients for U.S. airlines striving to meet the challenges of getting cargo, mail, and passengers to all corners of the continent and, increasingly, the world.

For a while the challenge would be met—but then the world would change again.

Historical Headlines:

THE 1960s

1961	April 12. In an orbital space flight Soviet cosmonaut Yuri Gagarin becomes first human in space. May 5. In a suborbital flight, Alan Shepard becomes the first American in space. The United States begins direct military support to South Vietnam, in the form of two helicopter units.
1962	John Glenn becomes the first American to make an orbital flight in space.
1963	Civil rights demonstrations take place throughout the nation. Medgar W. Evers, a civil rights leader, is shot and killed in Jackson, Mississippi. President John F. Kennedy is assassinated. His suspected assassin, Lee Harvey Oswald, is murdered by Jack Ruby, a nightclub owner. Vice President Lyndon Baines Johnson becomes president.
1964	Reports of North Vietnamese attacks on U.S. gunboats in the Gulf of Tonkin form the basis for expanded U.S. involvement in the war in Vietnam. A 17.6-mile highway ocean crossing, the Chesapeake Bay Bridge-Tunnel, is completed. November. The Verrazano-Narrows Bridge between Brooklyn and Staten Island, New York, the longest suspension span in North America, is completed.
1965	U.S. troops are sent to Vietnam. Antiwar demonstrations and civil rights demonstrations take place.
1966	The U.S. Department of Transportation is established at cabinet level. This year 78 million passenger cars and 16 million trucks and buses are registered.
1968	The United States and Vietnam hold peace talks in Paris, and the United States ends bombing in North Vietnam. Dr. Martin Luther King, Jr., black civil rights leader, is assassinated. Senator Robert F. Kennedy is assassinated in Los Angeles.
1969	Neil Armstrong and Buzz Aldrin become the first men on the Moon.

9

TRIUMPHS AND TROUBLES: NEWER, BIGGER, BETTER VERSUS AGE: THE 1970s, 1980s and 1990s

By 1970 aviation had come a long way since that cold December day at Kitty Hawk. The big airlines served every major city, and several international airports, such as O'Hare in Chicago, Los Angeles, Seatac in Seattle-Tacoma, San Francisco, Oakland, New York and Miami, served as jumping-off points for flights throughout the world. Even small towns of 2,000 to 5,000 people had airports to serve chartered flights and private planes. And most medium-size towns were connected by networks of "puddle-jumpers," commuter air lines, such as Ozark Air Lines, which linked points like St. Louis with Columbia, Missouri and Kansas City, or Pacific Southwest Airlines, which connected the San Francisco Bay Area with Fresno, California, Burbank and other points south. People began to talk about "bicoastal" life styles, even commuting between New York and Los Angeles. Flight had done more to connect the continent from east to west and north to south—and to the rest of the world—than any other transportation system ever before, transforming the way Americans shipped, lived, did business and spent their vacations. The coming decades would see even more changes in a maturing industry. By the end of the 1970s, government deregulation of the airlines altered the entire shape of the industry and affected the costs of air travel. Meanwhile, issues

of safety and security would become increasingly important as the nation's air fleet began to age and as more and more hijackings occurred. And new aircraft would continue to ply the skies.

DEREGULATION—1978

Since passage of the Civil Aeronautics Act of 1938, which created a national Civil Aeronautics Authority (later the Civil Aeronautics Board, or CAB) to regulate the airlines, no piece of legislation affected the growth of U.S. airlines as greatly as the Airline Deregulation Act of 1978. Now the CAB's broad authority to regulate routes, fares, and entry of new air carriers into the market was suddenly, dramatically transformed. In response to the 1978 legislation, by October 1980 the board had created new categories of carriers, including: Majors (with over $1 billion annual revenues), Nationals (between $75 million and $1 billion in revenues), Large Regionals, Medium Regionals and Other (mostly charter companies).

The Majors in 1980 included familiar names: American, Braniff, Continental, Delta, Eastern, Northwest, Pan American, Republic, Trans World (TWA), United, USAir and Western. From 1938 to

1977 competition among the airlines revolved around service and performance—getting there faster, more comfortably, or more pleasantly. The CAB decided every other aspect of their business. But with deregulation, everything was up for grabs—market entry, exit, and fares could be juggled to wield against competitors. Many airlines engaged in price wars and aggressively wooed the frequent business flyer as well as the vacation traveler. Cargo transportation also became keenly competitive. Complex factors came into play for airline managers. As one industry observer, John Newhouse, put it, in the new marketplace "Managing an airline is one of the more inexact sciences." By 1991 many of the 12 Majors of 1980 had suffered financial setbacks, fallen by the wayside or gone through a new set of mergers, including Braniff, Eastern, Continental and Pan Am. Many of the smaller airlines also suffered.

The CAB, however, has jurisdiction only over interstate commerce. Airlines operating solely within any state are regulated by state law—a phenomenon important primarily in California, Florida and Texas. Intrastate air carriers such as Pacific Southwest Airlines (PSA) had operated for a long time without federal government regulation of procedure, equipment, routes or fares. Some such carriers, of course, have come and gone very fast; consider Pacific Air Lines, which was founded in April 1946 and bankrupt by the end of 1947. Even for intrastate flight, though, the marketplace of the 1980s and 1990s provides a severe test. PSA, for example, founded in 1949, flew its last flight before the end of the 1980s.

Nonetheless, by the mid-1980s, air passenger service was again setting new records. Despite the problems faced by the industry, 313 billion paid passenger miles were flown on major U.S. airlines in 1986.

ACCIDENTS AND AN AGING FLEET

On February 25, 1989 headlines proclaimed "Big Hole in Fuselage—9 Vanish Over Pacific," "Deadly 'Hurricane' Inside 747" and "Terror in the Sky." "All

This gaping hole ripped open on the side of a Boeing 747 headed out of Honolulu, forcing it to return to the airport. Nine lives were lost. AP/Wide World Photos

On March 3, 1991, 25 passengers were killed when this United Airlines flight crashed near Colorado Springs. AP/Wide World Photos

of a sudden there was a terrible whooshing sound across the aisle and a big noise. When I looked over there everybody was gone," one passenger told reporters. "It was horrible," another passenger said. "All of a sudden the man next to Susan [another passenger] just disappeared."

Just 20 minutes after taking off from Honolulu Airport on its way to New Zealand, the big United Airlines Boeing 747 jet had suddenly, inexplicably, lost a door at 23,000 feet. Nine of the 354 passengers aboard were reported missing, apparently sucked out of the cabin by the sudden change in air pressure. The pilot succeeded in returning the aircraft to Honolulu for a safe emergency landing, and the lives of the remaining passengers were saved. But once again attention focused on the question of aircraft safety.

The airline industry has always taken flight safety seriously, and with good reason. When an airplane crashes, it creates headlines. Usually the tragedy is dramatic, the passengers are helpless and, unlike that morning in February 1989, most or all of them die in the accident. The effect on ticket sales can be devastating.

The first major airline accident in U.S. flight history occurred on June 30, 1956 when a TWA Super-Constellation collided with a United DC-7 over the Grand Canyon in Arizona. One hundred twenty-eight people died in the crash. Over the next 30 years, some 56 major air disasters (involving 100 or more fatalities) occurred. Most of the worst accidents, though, did not occur in the United States until May 1979, when a Douglas DC-10 crashed while taking off from Chicago's O'Hare Airport. It was the worst U.S. air disaster to date, resulting in the deaths of 258 passengers and 13 crew members, a total of 271 people. Five years earlier another DC-10 had crashed just after takeoff from Orly Airport in Paris, killing all 345 people on board. A third DC-10 crashed in late 1979 over Antarctica. As a result of the crashes, U.S. authorities grounded the DC-10s until the aircraft's structural soundness could be checked and cleared.

As more and more people fly daily, with more and more aircraft in the air at one time or taking off and landing, naturally, more and more accidents occur. By the early 1970s the rate of accidents had risen to one in every 400,000 flying hours—a rate seen as unacceptable even to those inside the industry. With the advent of the jumbo jets, the effects of a single crash can be especially tragic. Nearly 600 people were

Inside a Boeing 757 or 767 cockpit. Boeing

killed when two Boeing 747s collided at Tenerife Airport in the Canary Islands in 1977, and more than 500 died in a 747 crash outside of Tokyo in 1985. And by 1980 more than 1,000 jumbo jets had entered service around the world.

The causes of air disasters are varied and complex—ranging from structural problems, to human error, to sabotage. But authorities such as the Federal Aviation Administration (FAA), aircraft manufacturers and the airlines themselves have worked hard to discover the causes and eliminate them wherever possible.

With literally dozens of aircraft arriving and departing from busy airports at one time, air traffic control has become vitally important in preventing accidents. Air traffic control coordinates the flight plans of all aircraft departing from an airport, informs pilots of weather conditions on the ground, allocates an airway to the aircraft and tracks it by radar. An aircraft flying along an airway (which, like a highway, has an assigned number) travels at an assigned altitude, passing from one control zone to another until it arrives at its destination. There the pilot receives information from the controller about weather conditions in the air and on the runway, instructions about approach and landing, and advice about whether to use automatic instruments for landing. Landing, taxiing and takeoff are guided visually by an air traffic controller high above the runway in the control tower.

With over 80% of all accidents caused by human error, airlines have emphasized crew training and installed extensive instrumentation and automatic, computerized functions in their aircraft. A glimpse at the flight deck of a contemporary jetliner and its mass of dials and switches reveals how complex a job the crew faces. Since many accidents occur either at takeoff or landing, automatic equipment has been developed to reduce the possibility of human error at these critical points in the flight.

Ever since two de Havilland Comet jets disintegrated in 1954, passengers have recognized the possibility that faulty design or shoddy manufacture can cause an aircraft to fail—with disastrous results. In recent years, concern has risen about the effects of inadequate maintenance and metal fatigue as well. To explain what causes a crash, airliners carry onboard recorders, often referred to as the "little black box," which record data from all the aircraft's instruments as well as voice remarks by the crew. Even when the entire crew is lost, voice recorders retrieved from the wreckage can help investigators understand what occurred at the time of an accident—with the aim of preventing the same kind of accident from happening again.

SECURITY ON THE AIRWAYS

The first airplane ever to be hijacked, as far as the records show, was a Fokker F-7 in Peru around 1930—so hijacking isn't really new. But in recent years hijacking and sabotage have become more frequent and, of course, with the increase in the number of passengers on board, even more tragic. A bomb smuggled aboard a 747 jetliner en route from London to New York on December 21, 1988 exploded over Lockerbie, Scot-

land and killed 270 people. Hundreds of hijackings have occurred since World War II, with more than half a dozen significant incidents on flights originating in the United States. As a result, security in airports the world over has been stepped up considerably since 1972. Magnetometers were installed in airports to detect metal objects either on the person or in the carry-on luggage of all boarding passengers. Airport officials have received broad powers to search and detain suspects. Due to increased security many sabotage and hijacking plans have been foiled.

BUILDING AIRCRAFT FOR THE 1990s

The 1970s were heyday years for aircraft manufacturers in America, with unit sales in 1978 mounting to an all-time high of 18,962. Most of those, however, were general aviation aircraft (small planes). Overall, industry watchers see the years between the end of World War II and 1978 as the golden years of aircraft manufacturing in the United States. "The legacy of World War II," according to Artemis March, writing for *Technology Review* in December 1990, "was production capability, project management, and engineering skills, and rather than coasting on those assets, U.S. aviation companies built on them. They thought long-term, developed global products and product support, and repeatedly bet their companies on major

---

Round the World on One Tank: The Flight of the Voyager

Reminiscent of feats of such early aviation heroes as Orville and Wilbur Wright, Charles Lindbergh and Amelia Earhart, the flight of the *Voyager* was a triumph of individual human ingenuity and daring over natural forces that had seemed to say "it can't be done." On December 14, 1986 Richard G. Rutan and Jeanna Yeager took off from Edwards Air Force Base in southern California in a graceful two-seater designed by Rutan's brother, Burt, and built to his specifications. Since the 1970s, Burt Rutan had been designing small aircraft, pioneering with all-composite construction (lightweight manmade materials such as Kevlar) and the use of small computers (he started out using one of the early Apple personal computers). *Voyager* was a one-of-a-kind aircraft specially designed to carry twice its weight in fuel. Now, flying at an average speed of 116 miles per hour, Dick Rutan and Yeager made the first nonstop around-the-world flight without refueling. Their 25,012-mile journey almost doubled the previous unrefueled distance record, as they glided in for a landing on December 23. Rutan and Yeager emerged from their cramped seats jubilant if tired. They had not only set a record, but they had proven the viability of Burt Rutan's all-composite aircraft under every conceivable flight condition.

A McDonnell Douglas MD-11 Trijet. Douglas Aircraft Company

technological jumps," such as the Boeing 747. But in 1978 deregulation changed all that. Now that airline formation and fares were no longer controlled, new airlines could enter the marketplace economically by buying old equipment and still turn a profit while charging lower fares. The major airlines had to cut costs dramatically in order to compete and could no longer afford to invest in cutting-edge technology. Also, as they were no longer assured of specific routes, even the majors were less likely to place early orders for new models. This removed the long-term commitment that aircraft manufacturers needed to finance research and development.

In Europe, meanwhile, a consortium of countries had formed Airbus Industrie, which introduced its first aircraft in 1974. Although success came slowly to Airbus, by 1977 even U.S. airlines had begun to buy its planes. By mid-1987 Airbus deliveries had mounted to $21.9 billion, with backlogged orders amounting to $12 billion. The U.S. aircraft industry has complained about the "unfair advantage" Airbus has, thanks to the degree that consortium governments subsidize Airbus, but the fact remains that a constellation of circumstances have dramatically changed the U.S. aircraft marketplace.

By 1986 sales of commercial transport aircraft in the United States had reached an all-time high of $10.5 billion. Some 46.6% of the orders in this category in 1986 were from foreign airlines—indicating a favorable balance of trade in the civil aircraft end of the aircraft manufacturing industry. General aviation airplane sales, however, are hurt by strong foreign competition, the high cost of product liability insurance and the abundance of lower cost used aircraft.

As international traffic—both passenger travel and cargo—has increased in the 1990s, along with the economic pressures created by deregulation, the aircraft manufacturers have striven to meet the demand for more fuel-efficient planes with larger capacity. The McDonnell Douglas MD-11 is a good example. This $100 million aircraft can seat 251 people and fly nonstop between California and Tokyo. By contrast, the earlier DC-10 carries fewer passengers and uses significantly more fuel for the same trip. In fact, a DC-10 taking off for Asian flights from northern California's San Jose Airport, where the longest runway is only 8,900 feet, has to make a puddle jump to Oakland (less than 30 miles away, where the runways are longer) to pick up the extra fuel it needs for the flight. The MD-11, however, can take off from San Jose

Historical Headlines

1970s–1990s

1970	Paris Peace Talks between the United States and Vietnam continue, with increased public pressure to end war.
1973	The United States and South Vietnam sign a cease-fire with North Vietnam; the Vietnam War ends.
1974	Richard Nixon, plagued by the Watergate scandal, resigns as president of the United States.
1976	Gasoline shortages during winter months reduce use of automobiles.
1977	Energy crisis continues in the United States.
1978	New Panama Canal treaties are ratified, giving control of the canal to Panama at the end of 1999 and the United States the right to defend the canal's neutrality.
1979	The United States suspends Iranian oil imports in response to holding of 50 American hostages in Iran; energy crunch continues.
1980	The U.S. population reaches more than 226,500,000.
1981	U.S. hostages in Iran are released.
	About 13,000 air traffic controllers go on strike.
1981–82	Recession in the United States.
1983	October. U.S. troops land in Grenada, intervening in a coup there.
	Thousands of independent truckers go on strike in protest against increased fuel taxes.
1986	The United States launches nighttime air attacks against Libya in a tense standoff.
1989	Earthquake in San Francisco severely damages San Francisco–Oakland Bay Bridge and freeway in Oakland.
	East Germany tears down the Berlin Wall, ending the "Cold War" period of antagonism and noncooperation between the Soviet Bloc and the West (including the United States).
1990	Iraq attacks Kuwait, causing another hike in gasoline and oil prices in the the United States.
1990–91	Recession in the United States.
1991	United Nations military forces push Iraq out of Kuwait.

and fly directly to Tokyo without the pit stop. The advantage makes international flights from smaller airports more viable than ever before. Extended-range versions of the MD-11, which first flew in 1990, are capable of flying 8,870 miles.

By the 1990s many smaller cities had international airports, with overseas flights departing from such cities as San Jose and Sacramento, California. By 1991 United Air Lines began pressuring Boeing to develop an even bigger jumbo jet—one that could carry 650 passengers—to serve its long-distance international flights. And greater fuel efficiency in aircraft continues to be a major objective of airplane manufacturers. As the first century of powered, controlled flight draws to a close, the future holds continued change for airline operators, aircraft manufacturers, airports and airways—both challenges and opportunities for continued growth.

Air Facts

1970s to 1990s

1976 Pan-American makes the world's longest nonstop commercial airline flight, 8,088 miles, in 13 hours 31 minutes.

1978 The Airline Deregulation Act of 1978 transforms the civil aviation marketplace by reducing the powers of the Civil Aeronautics Board and restoring regulation of fares to the airlines.

1979 The worst U.S. air disaster occurs when an American Airlines DC-10 crashes on takeoff, killing 275 people.

1986 December 14–23. Richard Rutan and Jeanna Yeager pilot *Voyager*, a two-seater airplane designed by Burt Rutan, around the world on a record nonstop unrefueled flight, a distance of 25,012 miles.

1989 February 25. Nine passengers die when a door detaches from a United Air Lines Boeing 747 in flight over the Pacific Ocean.

APPENDIX

Major Events in U.S. Air Transport

1903	December 17. Orville and Wilbur Wright make the first successful manned flight of a motorized aircraft at Kitty Hawk, North Carolina.
1911	Cal Rodgers makes the first transcontinental solo flight.
1917	U.S. Post Office establishes air mail service.
1919	Daily air mail service begins between New York City and Chicago.
1926	Air Commerce Act of 1926 results in civil airfields with lights, licensing of pilots and other federal regulations.
	First scheduled and sustained passenger air service in the United States, from San Francisco to Los Angeles, is begun by Western Air Express.
1927	Charles Lindbergh makes the first transatlantic solo flight, fueling American enthusiasm for flight.
	The first transcontinental passenger flight.
1937	The *Hindenburg* dirigible bursts into flames as it lands in Lakehurst, New Jersey, killing 36 people.
1947	Los Angeles Airways opens the first scheduled helicopter service (mail delivery).
1949	First flight of a Boeing Stratocruiser, introducing luxury passenger travel by air.
	First prototype "big jet" airliner, the Boeing 707, is introduced.
1956	First major airline accident: A United DC-7 and a TWA Constellation collide over the Grand Canyon, killing all passengers, 128 people.
1961	April 12. In an orbital space flight Soviet cosmonaut Yuri Gagarin becomes first human in space.
	May 5. In a suborbital flight, Alan Shepard becomes the first American in space.
1962	John Glenn becomes first American to make an orbital space flight.
1966	U.S. Department of Transportation is established at cabinet level.

1969   Neil Armstrong and Buzz Aldrin become the first men on the moon.

1976   Pan-American makes the world's longest nonstop commercial airline flight, 8,088 miles in 13 hours 31 minutes.

1977   Energy crisis continues in the United States.

1978   Deregulation Act of 1978 removes federal regulation of airline fares.

1979   In the worst U.S. air disaster, an American Airlines DC-10 loses an engine on takeoff and crashes in Chicago, killing all 272 people on board and three on the ground.

    The United States suspends Iranian oil imports in response to holding of 50 American hostages in Iran; energy crunch continues.

1981   About 13,000 air traffic controllers go on strike.

1990   Iraq attacks Kuwait, causing another hike in gasoline and oil consumer prices in the United States.

GLOSSARY

aerodynamics The science that studies the motion of air around objects and the forces it exerts on them, including resistance, drag, pressure, and so on.

aileron A movable hinged section of an airplane wing, at the tip or on the trailing edge; used to control rolling tenencies.

airboat Aircraft capable of landing and taking off on water.

air controller Individual who directs air traffic at an airport, usually from a tower.

amphibious aircraft Aircraft capable of landing and taking off on both land and water.

balloon An unsteerable craft made of a nonporous bag of light material filled with hot air or a gas that is lighter than air. The hot air or gas rises, causing the balloon and its attached basket of passengers to rise.

barnstorm (v.) To perform air acrobatics or carry passengers on unscheduled sightseeing tours, especially in rural areas.

biplane An airplane with two wings, one above the other.

boatplane Same as an airboat.

cockpit Space in the fuselage of an airplane for the pilot, or, in large passenger planes, for the pilot and crew.

drag (n.) A force that slows an airplane's motion.

dirigible A lighter-than-air craft, or balloon, having propulsion and steering systems.

flap A movable area on an airplane wing's trailing edge that can be used to increase drag or lift.

fuselage The main body of an airplane, used to carry crew and passengers or cargo.

general aviation aircraft Aircraft not used for commercial or military purposes.

glider A heavier-than-air aircraft with no engine.

heavier-than-air Describes an aircraft that does not float in air naturally and must rely on engine power and/or aerodynamic design for lift.

hydrogen A gas that is lighter than air.

internal combustion engine An engine that derives its power from combustion that occurs inside the engine itself, not in an external furnace.

jet engine An airplane engine that propels the plane by creating hot gases that shoot out from the rear of the engine and push the plane forward.

leading edge The forward edge of a wing.

lift (n.) A force that increases an airplane's upward motion.

lighter than air Describes an aircraft that weighs less than the air around it and so rises naturally without the use of additional power.

monoplane An airplane having one set of wings.

pontoon A float on an airplane that enables it to land and take off on water.

powered flight Flying with the use of an engine in addition to aerodynamic forces. Powered flight enables longer flights.

propeller A device that uses a system of blades rotating around a central hub to propel an airplane.

seaplane An airplane designed to take off and land on water (same as a boatplane).

tailplane The horizontal portion of a plane's tail, providing stability.

trailing edge The back edge of the wing.

wind tunnel A passageway that is used in testing airplane design. A model of an airplane is placed inside the passage and air is sent through the tunnel at a known velocity to test the effects of air movement and wind pressures.

BIBLIOGRAPHY

Bilstein, Roger E. *Flight Patterns: Trends of Aeronautical Development in the United States, 1918–1929*. Athens, Ga.: University of Georgia Press, 1984.

———. *Flight in America: From the Wrights to the Astronauts*. Baltimore: The Johns Hopkins University Press, 1987.

Bruchey, Stuart. *The Wealth of the Nation: An Economic History of the United States*. New York: Harper & Row, 1988.

Chamberlain, John. *The Enterprising Americans: A Business History of the United States*. New York: Harper & Row, 1963.

———, and Frances. *The Ingenious Yankees*. New York: Thomas Y. Crowell, 1976.

Encyclopedia of Aviation. New York: Charles Scribner's Sons, 1977.

Groner, Alex. *American Business and Industry*. New York: American Heritage, 1972.

Heyn, Ernest V. *Fire of Genius: Inventors of the Past Century*. Garden City, N.Y.: Doubleday, 1976.

Holbrook, Stewart H. *The Yankee Exodus*. New York: Macmillan, 1950.

Lingeman, Richard. *Small Town America*. New York: G. P. Putnam's Sons, 1980.

Merk, Frederick. *History of the Westward Movement*. New York: Alfred A. Knopf, 1978.

New Jersey Department of Transportation. *The Development of Transportation in New Jersey*. Newark, N.J.: NJDOT, 1975.

Schlesinger, Arthur M., Jr., ed. *The Almanac of American History*. New York: G. P. Putnam's Sons, 1983.

Schonenberger, William A., with Paul Sonnenburg. *California Wings: A History of Aviation in the Golden State*. Produced in cooperation with the California State Chamber of Commerce. Woodland Hills, Calif.: Windsor Publications, 1984.

Smelser, Marshall, and Joan R. Gundersen. *American History at a Glance*, 4th ed. New York: Harper & Row, 1978.

Urdang, Laurence, ed. *The Timetable of American History*. New York: Simon & Schuster, 1981.

INDEX

Italic numbers indicate illustration.